Gary Paulsen

with illustrations by
Ruth Wright Paulsen

FATHER WATER, MOTHER WOODS

Essays on
Fishing and Hunting
in the North Woods

Published by
Bantam Doubleday Dell Books for Young Readers
a division of
Bantam Doubleday Dell Publishing Group, Inc.
1540 Broadway
New York, New York 10036

The trademark Laurel-Leaf Library® is registered in the U.S. Patent and
Trademark Office.
The trademark Dell® is registered in the U.S. Patent and Trademark Office.

ISBN: 0-440-21984-1

RL: 7.4

Reprinted by arrangement with Delacorte Press

Printed in the United States of America

April 1996

10 9 8 7 6 5 4 3 2

OPM

This book is dedicated to the memory of Nick Allemenos,
a casualty of our times.

Contents

Camping

Hunting

Foreword

In the thirty to forty thousand letters a year that come asking about *Hatchet* there are many diversities—questions about Brian, how his life is getting on, how he likes high school, is he old enough now to get married, have children; some readers have even done videos depicting different aspects of Brian's life, and more than once media has asked where he lives so he could be interviewed for magazines or papers.

But there is one thread that permeates nearly all the letters.

Almost without exception there is an overwhelming desire to know how it all started, where *Hatchet* began.

It is a simple question, but like so many simple questions it has a complex answer. The knowledge that went into writing *Hatchet* came from my life, and the forces that shaped and guided that life started not in the woods but in the throes of alcoholism.

I was one of the wasted ones.

The ones who turned away.

It was before foster homes or attempts to understand and help children from "problem" families; before machinery existed to catch young people who fell through the cracks, dropped by the wayside, were lost in the mist, and all those other cliches that are applied to familial casualties—the young walking wounded of the society. I was one of them, one of the emotionally injured, who awakened crying in the night, the boys who saw with wide eyes and could say nothing.

In those days, there were no programs to help, no government agencies, but the problems were still there; the abuse and alcohol and emotional strain and pain—all existed then and before then, except that when a young person had trouble, there wasn't any way to fix it. The young would either have to stand and take it, which many did, to great and lasting harm, or they could cut and run.

I ran to the woods and rivers of northern Minnesota.

It was, I suppose, a kind of self-fostering—perhaps a subconscious seeking of help from nature—although we did not think of it in those terms. It was simpler. In the normal run of things our lives hurt. When we were in the woods or fishing on the rivers and lakes our lives didn't hurt. We did what didn't hurt, and as it didn't hurt more and more, we spent more and more time in the woods and on the rivers—a natural flow of survival.

It also, in a very direct way, led to the novel *Hatchet* for it was there, on the soft winding rivers and quiet blue lakes, in the quick splash of fall color, the hiss of line going off a reel, the soft crack of an old .22 rifle sighted on grouse (fool hen), the shaking hands that aimed at first deer with a straight bow and homemade arrows—it was there that *Hatchet* was born.

Fishing

Down by the
Power Dam

Every year it is necessary for fishing to start. Even though it has gone on year-round it must have a beginning each year, and fishing always started in the spring.

In the small northern town in Minnesota where we were raised it is possible that everything started in the spring, but fishing was the most important thing, and it became vital to watch for the signs that it would begin.

There were two primary indications.

One was the car on the ice.

Pollution was not then considered nor discussed, and each year the town would put an old car on the frozen ice of the river and tie wires from the car to a clock on a tree on the bank. The idea was that when the ice started to go out the car would fall through the ice, trip the clock, and there would be an exact record of when this event occurred.

Much was made of this whole business. It was not just a way to dispose of old cars—although over the years the bottom of the river became littered with them, and God only knows how many fishing lures were lost by people trying to fish around the cars and catching their hooks on door handles or bumpers. More importantly, the old car on the ice became a contest that occupied the whole town.

Everybody guessed at the exact moment when the ice would progress enough into the "rotten" stage (also known as "honeycomb ice," which I would come to know intimately and with horror later, running dog teams on small lakes and the Bering Sea) and allow the car to drop to the bottom.

It started that simply. At the courthouse or the library there was a large bulletin board, and for a dollar you could sign the board and write down your guess to win the car-through-the-ice raffle. Of course, you never met anyone who had won, but only those who knew somebody who had won, and therein, in the winning, the simplicity was lost.

The raffle dominated the town. Merchants competed with each other to put up prizes for the winner so that along with a sizable cash award there were dozens, hundreds of other prizes, and all of them had to do with summer and most of them had to do with fishing.

Rods, reels, life jackets, lures, anchors, boats, picnic baskets, motors—it was said that a person could win the raffle and be set for life as far as fishing or summer was concerned, and as the time approached people would find reasons to walk or drive along the river to see the old car.

"Oh, I had to run down to the elevator and check on grain prices," they would say. "The car has one wheel through but she's still hanging there."

"My aunt's been feeling poor," they would say, about an aunt they hadn't spoken to in twelve years, "and I thought I should stop by and check on her. The car has both rear wheels down now. She's just hanging there, teetering . . ."

"Your aunt?"

"No, the car, you ninny—the car on the ice."

And as the time grew still closer there were those who would come and sit with bottles in paper sacks and fur caps and boogers hanging out their noses and drink and spit and scratch and wait and sometimes pray; just sit there and wait for the car to fall and make their fortunes.

Naturally it never happened when anybody thought it would happen, but it always signaled the end, the final end of winter.

And the beginning of spring. Also, when the ice became that rotten it began the signal to the fish that spawning was close.

The second indication was the light.

All winter the light had been low, flat, cold. In midwinter it became light in the morning at nine or so and began to get dark at three-thirty or four in the afternoon on a cloudy day, and most of the time it seemed to be dark and cold.

But as spring came and the ice became rotten on the river the light moved, was a thing alive. The sun came back north, like an old friend that seemed to have been gone forever, and it changed everything, changed the way things looked. There was still snow, still cold at night, but during the day it was brighter, clearer; everything seemed bathed in soft gold.

People changed as well. During the winter, talk —what talk there was—was always short and to the point and almost always seemed to be on weather-related problems: how difficult it was to start a car in the cold, who was sick with a cold, who was getting sick, who had been sick and was getting well only to get sick again, how it was necessary to drain the car radiators at night (this was before antifreeze) and refill them with warm water when it was time to start them the next day and how they almost never started and wasn't it a shame that the car companies, the Car Companies with all their money, couldn't design a car to start in the winter?

The light changed all that, made the winter end, though there was still more cold weather, still more mornings when nostril hairs stuck to the insides of your nose and the combed ducktails froze on the way to school, more days when it was possible to play the joke where somebody talks somebody else —and where do they keep coming from, the ones who can be talked into these things?—into pushing their tongue out on a frozen propane tank where it would stick and leave a piece of tongue-skin.

The light changed all things.

It was the same sun, and it seemed to come up at the same time, but it rose higher and made gold, new gold that altered everything. Jacobsen's Bakery, where we would get free fresh hot rolls sometimes in the morning to carry when we delivered papers— two rolls each, one in the mouth and one still hot in the pocket of the jacket for later—the bakery was transformed. It had been an old brick building with a loading ramp on the back for the truck to get the fresh bread, and now, in the new gold light it became a bright castle of fresh-bread smells and beauty rising out of the alley next to the Montgomery Ward (always, always called the Monkey Wards) store.

The trees near the library, still without leaves, still with scrabbly arms that reached into the sky, did not seem ominous now but reaching. And the library seemed to shine with warmth and beckoned in the new light, and it became impossible to believe in winter any longer, only in the newness of spring.

And fishing.

For a moment, a day, a week—for a time that felt forever, everything hung, balanced on the edge.

The car . . . didn't . . . *quite* . . . fall through the ice, the light promised but spring did not seem to come, the trees tried but didn't quite bud.

Just for a moment in the year. Just for a flick of time, everything hung and we would daily go to where the first signals would be, the first true movement of spring.

Down to the dam.

The river wound through town without any purpose, a lazy snake. It seemed to barely move as it crawled beneath the Ninth Street bridge, an eighth of a mile wide, past the swimming beach, and under the First Street bridge approaching the dam.

Here it changed. At the south end of town, years before, they had put a dam straight across the whole river. It was made with two floodgates that could be lowered or raised with large screw-wheels, and at the side, over a wide spillway, they had erected a power plant.

The backed-up river fought to get through the spillway and in so doing turned two large, whining turbines that furnished electricity to the town, and none of this mattered to us when the light changed and the car came near to falling through the ice.

At the lower end of the building housing the turbines the water came out in a spillway. With the whine of the turbines mixing into the thundering roar of the water pounding out of the spillway it was difficult to hear anything but the dam, the power of it.

But when the sun rose high enough to bring the soft light into the recesses of the spillway, or perhaps it was because there was a smell to the rotting of the ice on the river or the way the sun hit the ice—for whatever reason, the fish began to dance.

Old rhythms, old, very old music drove them. For all the time there is, the fish have run in the spring, and they have memory built into their genes, of being born upstream, always upstream, and their parents and their grandparents and their great-grandparents—all have the same memory coded into them.

When the light was just so and the smell was just so, they must run, they must dance, they must get back upstream to lay eggs and fertilize them, and it does not matter that man has put the dam there to stop them, does not matter that there is the whirling death of the turbine there to shred and destroy them.

It was a thing to see, this dance, this run—a thing almost not to be believed. Carp, sheepshead, suckers, walleyes, and northern pike—all made the run, or tried to. Not at once. There is timing that has been worked out over the ages so that first the walleyes and northerns, then the carp and suckers, each in its turn tried, separated only by days, but separate.

And they could not make it.

None of them could get through the turbines. Even if they could in some way swim against the horrendous speed of the water being driven out of the spillway, the blades of the turbine would destroy them, and above that there was a mesh screen that would stop them.

They were completely doomed to failure, and yet each spring they tried to make the run and the dance and the water became alive with them. The spillway was perhaps thirty feet across and six or seven feet deep and when the run was on, the water was filled with fish rolling over one another, seething and fighting to get up to the turbines; but even that was difficult. Not just because of the speed of the water or the power of the force kicked out by the turbines, but because of the boys who had come to fish the run.

It was the first open-water fishing of the year and it was very important—as perhaps all fishing is very important.

There was great skill involved. Just getting to the water was a problem. Now and then a child fell into the spillway and was sucked downstream to drown, and be fished out miles later, and to keep that from happening, the town had put fencing around the dam and spillway. The fencing was elaborate. Chain link and steel pipes ten feet tall and angling out at the top to keep anyone from getting over, with barbwire at the very top to further discourage the boys, and none of it worked. It is possible that it slowed us, but only momentarily, and then we were over to hang on the outside of the fence, much more exposed to danger now than before because it was necessary to balance on a narrow ledge of concrete while clutching the fence with one hand and fishing with the other.

So many of us did this, climbed the fence and hung on the wires to fish, that sometimes it seemed a virtual net of lines went down into the water and it was a wonder any of the fish could get through.

It was not fishing in the pure sense of the word so much as snagging. While running, the fish don't eat—or nearly don't. Northerns will hit a lure now and then, but the others ignore bait and so it was necessary to snag them, which might seem crude, but there was an art to it.

Everything was done by feel, the feel of the line, the feel of the hook. The snag was a large triple-hook with a heavy sinker wired to the bottom of it with stovepipe wire, hung on the end of a steel leader and thirty-pound test line. All of this had to be done by hand because only one hand was available and it was impossible to use a rod and reel with one hand.

The hook had to be swung in a large arc up-stream to where the water pounded out of the spill-way, a looping arc just above the water, back and forth and back and forth, all with the movement of the arm and body while hanging onto the chain-link fence, out over the roaring water with the fingers clawed into the wire of the fence, always further and further until the hook and sinker drop just exactly, almost delicately, at the precise point the water exits the turbine.

It was here, fighting to get into the shredding turbines, that the mass of fish congregated, pushing and driving, rolling belly-over-back so thick there seemed to be no water between them.

Here the hook drops.

Just perfectly *here*.

Too deep and it falls below the seething fish into the rocky bottom of the spillway and is swept back beneath them; too shallow and it slides over their backs.

Perfect.

Once in ten, once in twenty tries it can be done right. Lean out, and out, so far as to nearly fall, then swing, again, again, and then finally, at last, the perfect toss.

The hook drops into the roiling mass of fish and water and begins moving back through them.

And it is here that practice, wisdom, patience, knowledge pay off. If the hook is jerked too soon, it won't be in the right place, will skid off the side or back of a fish and come up with nothing but silver scales stuck to it.

All by feel. The hook moves back through the fish and where it is, what the hook is doing, must be felt.

The line is wrapped around the hand, sometimes with a cheap cloth glove to keep it from cutting and the fingers cut off the glove so the line can be felt. The line leaves the hand out over the back of the index finger, lies across the finger so the movement of the hook can be sensed.

There are differences so subtle they cannot be told, cannot be taught—tiny bits of knowledge, of feeling, as fine and pure as those of any neurosurgeon.

The hook moves, bumping off fish, rolling down their sides, scraping; and all of it comes up through the line across the finger.

Until the hook nudges, ever so gently, into the nose of a fish, directly into the center of the nose. It hesitates slightly, seems to bounce, sends a live signal up through the line across the finger, and exactly then the hook must be jerked upward, with a sharp short motion, to set the hook into the lower jaw of the fish.

If one in twenty tries brings the hook into the right place, it is another one in twenty that the hook hits the nose right, lines up correctly, and angles the right way to allow the hook to set in the bony plate of the lower jaw.

The effect is electric.

The fish runs, cuts across the current so the power of the spillway is added to the power of the fish. If it is a large sheepshead or walleye, it is bad enough—the sudden lunge all comes into the hand wrapped in line. But if a northern pike is snagged, and set—twenty or more pounds—it can be nearly fatal. Not only is the line around the hand the only connection, the other hand is the only bond with the fence, and if the fish cuts out across the current, catches it right, swings back downstream, it pulls sideways at the hand so hard it is almost impossible to hang on and boys caught by surprise have been snatched from the wire and into the spillway to drown. But if it all works right, if all is perfect, there is the fish. Eight, ten, twenty pounds of northern or walleye or sheepshead or carp on the bank, swung out and wide with the free hand to land on the bank to be unhooked. And then the line is thrown back out, swinging, further and further.

Every bit of it completely illegal. It is the worst time to take fish, when they spawn, and once and sometimes twice a day the game warden comes by with a knife and cuts the lines and lets the hooks fall into the water and tells us if he catches us there again he will arrest us, but we know he is only saying that to scare us and when he is gone second hooks come out, or third or fifth—however many it takes.

There are too many things against the fish for them to win.

If they were just to eat, the fish, if they were just for food for the table for the boys, it might be all right to take them with snag hooks when they run, but it is not.

There is the whole winter against them, a whole winter of cold and dark, and so the fish, the running of them into the power plant, comes to mean more than just food.

It means the end of winter, the beginning of spring. The whole town talks of it.

"Are the fish running yet?" they ask. "Are they moving at the dam?"

And everybody wants to taste it, taste the spring with fresh fried fish dipped in batter and eaten with the last of the potatoes from the year before, taken up from the basement where they've been stored, and fried all crisp in butter with salt and pepper; or to strip the eggs from the fish into a frying pan with butter and fry them until they look like scrambled eggs.

The town lusts for the fish, and the boys who work the snag hooks are from poor families. There is no extra money, often no money at all, and so the fish became a part of how the boys live.

As soon as a fish was landed, a large one, the boy would run the two blocks from the dam to the center of uptown and hit the bars.

The Joliette Lounge, the Lumberjack Corner, the Woodsman Cafe and Beer Hall. Carp and suckers were not worth as much as the other fish and could be used only for smoking, which was good enough, if not the full freshness of spring, but northern pike and walleyes, if they were large enough, brought top money.

A nickel a pound.

Work the bars. The fish hanging on a piece of wire or twine; hit the front end of the bar, dark, smelling of stale beer and sweeping compound on the floor to soak up the spit and spill and puke, bars with grimy mirrors and no stools, only places to stand, with men leaning on their elbows, drinking from the tall brown-wet bottles—hit the front end and hold the fish out like a prize, a contest won.

"How much?" Beery breath, weaving men unshaven, hard to see in the dark of the bar.

"A dime."

"For the whole fish?"

How drunk *is* the son of a bitch? "No—a pound. He's a good one, go twelve, fifteen pounds. . . ."

"Hell, kid, he ain't ten."

"Come on—he's an easy twelve. . . ."

"Ten."

"Eleven."

Laughter, other men cutting in. "Hell, Swen, buy the damn fish. . . ."

And he bends. "All right, eleven pounds, a nickel a pound."

"A dime."

"That's it, kid—take a nickel or nothing. Feed it to your cat."

"I don't have a cat—seven cents."

"Damn, kid—all right. Six and that's it."

"Six. Times eleven pounds. That's sixty-six cents. . . ."

And at last the money, the pay, and then back to the dam at a run to find a place on the wire and unroll the line and start swinging the hook out and out to feel it come back, while another boy takes another fish to the bars to make money.

Sometimes riches—more money than can be imagined. Sometimes a huge fish—twenty pounds —and a drunk that forgets all the rules and pays the full dime a pound.

Two dollars.

Sometimes more—five, six fish in a day taken on the snag hooks at the dam, and a good day, the best day of all, the best day ever, earning nine dollars—a full day's pay for a grown man working for a dollar and a nickle an hour, which was the wage then, when boys made only two dollars and fifty cents and sometimes only a dollar a day doing mean-grunt work from sunup to sundown on the farms.

Nine dollars. Nine incredible dollars in one day to be jammed tightly into the pocket and hoarded and hidden from the larger boys and spent slowly on secret pleasures.

Candy, malts for a quarter and hamburgers, more candy until the belly bulges and then the next day back once more to the dam and the swinging hooks and the roaring water.

Spring and first fishing.

Working the
Ditches

S nagging fish below the dam was the
start of spring, but there were other,
different beginnings as well.

The country around the town was flat farmland,
the richest in the world, it was said, soil so black you
could see into it the way you see into a black mar-
ble, but flat, absolutely flat with no hills.

And no natural drainage.

The snow melts and the fields stand in water and
mud and would stand that way into summer because there is a clay base down a couple of feet that
won't allow the water to sink except for the ditches.

Somewhere in the past, in times before we were
born, great projects dug ditches for miles and miles
to drain the farms—some ditches thirty miles long,
straight through the farmlands, with side ditches
heading into networks of fields, so that on an aerial
photo hanging in the feed store, flyblown and

greasy, the ditches look exactly like the canals of Mars.

The fish do not know these are drainage ditches; they think they are creeks. After a time, some of them would nose up the ditches, in the spring when the runoff water was pouring out, push further and further up and lay eggs, and the spawning ground was imprinted on the new fish and then still more new fish until the ditches became an accepted spawning area for thousands and thousands of them.

Walleyes and northern pike run first, and because the snagging at the dam is going on at the same time, they are not bothered.

But after the walleyes and northerns come the suckers, and by that time the snagging at the dam is over. Then we would take spears or bows and work the ditches for suckers.

It was not easy. Using a spear with eight or ten tines it seemed impossible to miss, but the fish could move sideways, or appear to, and many times they were not where they seemed to be when the spear was jabbed. After a bit, a technique evolved— and for some reason it had to be relearned each year. The spear had to be held with the point in the water just over their backs and pushed forward and down almost delicately—too far and the spear would hit the rocks lining the bottom of the ditch and bend or break; too little and the spear would not penetrate far enough for the barbs to take hold.

Shooting them with a bow was also tricky at first. There were no fish arrows then to buy in the stores, and no money to buy them if they had been available. Bows were of lemonwood with fiber backing and arrows were homemade from cedar shafts that cost a nickel each and turkey feathers. A small hole could be drilled through the front of a field point and a tiny nail put through the hole and bent back to make a barb, then a forty-pound test fishing line was tied from another hole in the point back to the reel on the bow. The "reel" was a plastic water glass taped to the bow so that it tapered down to the front. The line had to be carefully wound on the glass each time, one wrap laid precisely next to the last so it would spin off (this was before spinning reels as well, which can be used now) without making the arrow fly off sideways.

It was all very involved, and if a shot was missed it might take five minutes to get ready for another one. For that reason we liked to get very close before shooting, and finally one boy found that you didn't need the reel or line at all. The ditch was shallow, and if you shot down, the arrow would go through the fish and pin them to the bottom.

There was no limit on suckers.

Gunnysacks were carried on a cord around the neck to drop the fish in when they were speared or shot, working up the ditch in the spring sunshine, walking in the icy water until our legs were blue— nobody could afford hip boots or waders—when we would stop and build a fire and warm feet and legs, working the ditches that way until the sacks weighed sixty or seventy pounds.

When the sack became too heavy to carry we would stop and use a pocketknife to gut all the fish, then continue on until even with gutted fish the weight was too much and the fish would be loaded on bicycles as a burro would be loaded, huge bags on the sides and top to push the miles home.

The suckers were not only for direct cooking and eating.

An old man—forty at least—had a smoke-shed set up on the edge of town. If you helped him, he would smoke your fish for half of them.

The suckers had to be split the long way down the back with a sharp knife and coarse salt hand-rubbed into the inside meat. Then they were hung over poles in the smoke-shed and a round-the-clock fire had to be made outside in the firepit. A buried stovepipe carried the smoke into the smoke-shed from the hardwood branches that were burned.

Hours turned to days turned to weeks—or so it seemed. The sucker run in the ditches lasted at most two weeks but it seemed much longer.

A constant procession of boys and bicycles moved from the ditches back into the old man's smoke-shed, and it did not matter that he was using the boys' work to get free fish, did not matter that we spent days with eyes burning from the smoke, spent days sitting in clouds of smoke, days and nights stoking and damping the fire to keep the smoke moving evenly through the racks of fish, did not matter that he kept half and maybe more than half to sell in the stores and at church suppers and to an endless line of cars that came to buy from him.

None of it mattered except the fish.

When they were done, when they were all shot with arrows and speared and gutted and carried and salted and smoked and at last were done, it was worth it.

First tastes were compared, measured against each other the way wine is compared.

The meat is soft-hard, gentle-leathery golden-brown, the color of caramel and deep honey mixed, and simply has to be eaten.

It comes off in strips, tastes delicately of salt and smoke—not of wood, but the taste of the smoke so that it seems that the forest itself is in the meat of the fish; a bite is like being there in the woods, a bite is part of a memory.

Except that the meat, the work in the meat, is too expensive to eat—the way farm workers cannot afford to eat the meat they grow and must instead eat venison and sell the beef and pork for money.

The fish must be sold, the work in the cold ditches must be sold.

If the taste of fresh cooked fish means spring to the town, the taste of fresh smoked fish means luxury.

Everybody wants it. There is no problem selling —we could sell ten times as much as we get. When we start down the street with the gunnysack the people find us, hunt us.

"How much?" they ask and it is not like in the bar with the snagged fish. No dickering.

"Fifty cents a side," we say. "Flat."

A nod and money. Half a fish, half a dollar—a dollar a fish, which sounds good, but to get a fish, one fish in the sack to sell, is a day at the ditch, another fish for the old man, nights working at the smoke-shed for the old man, and then . . . then to not eat the fish.

To *not* eat the fish.

To take a taste of the smoky-salt-golden-meat and then not eat the fish. . . .

Impossible.

It takes four, five fish to get just one to sell. Dreams of money, of wealth, die with a taste, one taste.

Pepsi for a nickel a bottle, two Pepsis and sit on the back porch of the apartment building while they drink and fight inside, two Pepsis and sit there and eat strips of smoked fish cut and washed down with cold Pepsi, eat until even the hair is greasy with it and every cat in the neighborhood is there with you, sitting there eating the fish in the spring sunshine and reading a Zane Grey western or an Edgar Rice Burroughs science fiction novel. . . .

No, not riches from selling the fish. Other riches, but not money from selling. Only fish to eat, to sit and read and eat.

Sometimes a dogfish is snagged or speared or shot. They are like an eel, long and wriggly with a fin that starts halfway down the back to wrap around the tail and up the belly. Most throw them away, consider them rough fish, but the old man at the smoke-shed knows a recipe, has secret salts and seasoning and smokes them. It is oily, almost greasy, and hard to eat at first—the first bite. But after that there is something there, some new edge of taste and we sit with the old man outside the smoke-shed and eat the dogfish—peeling long strips to lay on coarse bread and eat with strong hot tea sticky with sugar while the old man tells, weaves stories about fishing, smuggling booze across the Canadian border during Prohibition, stories of wild runs at night while federal agents shoot at the night-boats, glamorous stories of ugly things.

Spring ends there. . . .

Not in the ditches with cold blue legs, not at the power dam swinging the snag hook to bump the noses of the rolling fish nor in the bars hustling the drunks nor selling the smoked suckers on the street nor hiding on the back porch of the apartment to drink Pepsi and read and eat but there. . . .

At night by the smoke-shed eating the eellike dogfish and coarse bread and drinking hot tea, listening to old stories from the old man and petting the dog that eats all the bones and skin and heads from the smoked fish and is so fat his legs cannot hold him up for more than a few minutes at a time.

There.

Spring and first fishing end sitting by the smoke-shed on the soft nights as the buds turn to leaves even on the hardwoods and the stars lose their brittle winter look and take on the soft shape of summer, and the dog lays his head in a lap to beg and to be petted.

There it ends.

And summer begins.

First Strike

I n reality it is not possible to draw an exact line and say here one kind of fishing becomes another, just as it is not possible to draw an exact line in any part of life to separate it from another.

Summer fishing came in so many different forms, became so many different arts, that there must be a start to it, a beginning and a middle and an end just to be able to see it.

The start was where the river passed a smaller stream that entered the river by the Ninth Street bridge.

Though summer had come, always lying back hiding was the cold snap—a late killing frost that caught everybody off guard so often that it seemed people would come to expect it and not set their garden vegetables out. But they are always surprised by the frost, and have to wrap paper around the plants in small cones until the backyards of everybody in town seem to be full of buried elves with only their hats showing.

But the frost does more than kill plants. Something about it affects the fish, and where the stream comes into the river just after the frost and even during the frost the northern pike come to feed. It is perhaps that they think it is fall, or perhaps the cold makes small fish come there and the big ones follow.

And they are truly big—some of them like twenty-pound green sharks, filled with teeth and savagery.

Fishing for them was done one way and one way only—casting lures. Two lures worked the best, and everybody who came to work where the stream flows into the river used one or sometimes both of them. The best was a red-and-white daredevil—a spoon that is silver on one side with red and white stripes on the other and a single triple-hook at the bottom, or business end. The new ones didn't seem to work very well until they were scuffed and scratched by teeth tearing at the paint on them. Most of us tried rubbing them on rocks or concrete to scuff them up a bit, but it didn't work as well as having it done by teeth. The other lure was called a plug—a simple cylindrical piece of wood painted red in the front and white in the back with two small silver eyes and a "lip" made of stamped metal to pull the plug under when it was reeled in.

The rigs used then would not be considered usable by modern fishermen. This was all before glass or carbon rods and spinning reels or free-wheeling casting reels, and casting with them was a true art, a balance of coordination and luck. The line used was of a heavy braid—there were no monofilaments then either—rolled on a drum reel with thumb-busting side drive handles that had to spin with the drum when a cast was made.

Everything was in the thumb. The right thumb rested on the line drum, and the rod—a clunker made of spring steel and by modern standards about as flexible as casting with a tire iron—had to be whipped overhead and forward with great force at the same instant the thumb had to be lifted from the drum to allow the lure to pull the line out. But not all the way. If the thumb came up too much, the line would go too fast and cause a backlash—a tangle on the reel sometimes so hideous the line had to be cut from the drum with a pocketknife, hacked off, and replaced completely. But the thumb couldn't be pressed too hard either, or the lure wouldn't go anywhere.

And then, just as the lure entered the water the thumb had to act as a gentle brake and stop the line drum.

All to start just one cast.

And almost no casts produced a fish. It might take sixty or seventy casts to entice a northern to strike, and then it didn't always pay off.

If the daredevil was used it had to be allowed to wobble down into the water no more than a foot, and then the rod had to be put in the left hand and the right hand had to grip the handles, and the line had to be reeled in as fast as the hand could move to make the spoon roll and flip and flash silver and red. Then, just before shore the daredevil had to be stopped, cold, for half a second in case there was what was called a "follow-up" to give a fish time to hit it just then.

The plug was slightly different. Because it was of wood it floated and so the cast had time to be developed correctly. The cast could be placed with more time, the plug allowed to drift into position, and then the reeling started at one's leisure.

The lip on the front of the plug worked as a water scoop so that the faster the plug was reeled in the deeper it would dive, and the depth could be controlled that way. Some worked the tip back and forth to the right and left while reeling, but it didn't seem to help, just as spitting or peeing on the lure— another trick used by some—also didn't seem to help. Once somebody scrounged some blood from a butcher in a small bucket and dipped the lures in the blood, and that had some effect but made us stink for days of rotten blood and fish slime. It didn't bother us, but in school there was a noticeable reaction.

Again, as with the daredevil, when the plug was

close to shore it was stopped for half a moment to allow a possible follow-up strike, but really the cast was always everything. And though many—most—casts did not catch fish, each and every cast had to be made with art and skill and the hope, the prayer was always there that it would work; that *this* cast would work *this* time.

The problem was the cold. It was necessary to work the line in just the right place, reeling the braided line through the fingers to be able to "feel" when the first hit came, if it came. Braided line soaked up water, and this squeezed out on the finger, ran down the wrist, and dripped on the waist or legs—depending on where the reel was held.

Wet, cold hour after hour, each perfect cast followed by each perfect cast waiting for that moment, that split part of a moment when it comes.

The strike.

They are never the same. Daredevil strikes are different from plug strikes as cold-weather strikes are different from summer strikes, and every fish seemed to strike differently.

Northern pike are the barracuda of fresh water and when the mood is on them they will hit, tear at anything that moves. Mother loons keep their babies on their backs so the northerns won't get them, and baby ducks get nailed constantly. Northerns eat anything and everything. In their guts we found bottlecaps, can openers, cigarette lighters, bits of metal, nails, wire, pieces of glass and once, complete, a pair of sunglasses that fit one of the boys perfectly.

But they're picky. Not always, but sometimes. And they must be coerced, persuaded, into biting—begged, enticed.

A cast can be "dropped," the lure allowed to settle, then reeled in fast, then allowed to settle again and once more reeled fast—to make it seem sick or wounded. It can be skittered across the surface, then suddenly stopped, skittered and stopped, teased and teased, looking, waiting for *the* moment:

The strike.

It always comes like lightning. Sometimes there is just the tiniest hint, a small grating of their teeth on the lure as they come in for the hit, but usually there is no warning. One second the reel is turning and the lure is coming in, and the next there is a slashing blow and the line stops, begins to sizzle out, cuts the finger, and the rod bends, snaps down, and in some cases, if it is a large fish and a steel rod, it stays bent in a curve.

It is impossible to judge size. Three pounds seems like six, six like twelve and over. One cold, clear morning a miracle came. A cast, one clean cast with a daredevil that slipped into the water like a knife, clean and in and halfway back, the reel spinning as fast as it would go; there was a small grating on the lure and then a tremendous slashing strike, a

blow that nearly tore the rod away, and the line cut the water, sizzled off to the right so fast it left a wake.

Seventeen pounds.

A great green torpedo of a fish that tore the water into a froth, a fight that slashed back and forth until at last the fish was tired, until it nosed finally into the bank, where it could be dragged up onto the grass to lie, green and shining, the tail flapping, and a voice, a small voice notes the sadness of the fish and whispers in the mind and the words come out:

"Let it go."

"Are you crazy?"

"Let it go—it's too, too much fish to keep like this. Let it go. . . ."

"Nobody will believe it."

"We saw it. That's enough. Let him go."

And so it is.

Somebody has a scale, a spring with a needle that slides, and the fish is weighed, and the lure is removed, and it is laid in the shallows. It wiggles twice, a left and right squirm, and it's gone.

"It will learn," somebody says. "It will never strike again."

But he is wrong.

Four of us that day catch the same fish and release him, and each time he fights and each time he slides back into the river and disappears like a green ghost, and there are many other springs and thousands of other casts and hundreds of fish caught and eaten when it snaps cold where the stream comes into the river, but never the same again.

Never that same slamming surge of the first large strike.

Seventeen pounds.

Fishing for
Bulls

F ishing during the cold snap where the stream comes into the river is not always sure and is over in a short time, often only a day, two days, never more than a week, and is considered a small treat, a bonus for the boys who are purists.

There were other kinds of temporary fishing as well.

Just as the time for fishing starts, the panfish come into the shallows to spawn. These are not the later types of panfish to be caught in droves and bucketsful, but the first, the big ones that cannot be caught later because they stay deep, where it is impossible to get a lure or bait down to them through the clouds of small ones.

"Bulls," we call them. Not minnows or six-inch-long worm-eaters but truly large sunfish with flashing yellow bellies, bluegills over a pound, over two pounds, panfish to fight like northerns when they take the worm, and still, even with bait, even with a worm, there is art.

Nothing is left to chance, no part of the ritual is omitted. This was before anybody thought of fly-fishing for panfish, and the boys were too poor for the split-bamboo rods of that time anyway—and lures specifically for panfish (wigglers, small bugs, etc.) were far in the future. All to be had were the spring-steel casting rods and the thumb-busting early Shakespeare reels used for all fishing.

But there were ways to make the heavy gear act like lighter equipment.

A tiny hook was used and a small sinker set well above—two feet at least—a gut leader, a twist knot with the end fed through to tie the hook to the leader, many with different knots, so that there were always arguments about who had the better knot, who could hold the largest "bull" sunfish (actually females) with his knot; gear arguments that would go on all summer, go on all year, go on all of lives, though we could not see that then while we worked the shallows when the big sunfish and bluegills came in to spawn.

It is possible that the lure, the bait, the place-ment of it made no difference, but nobody believed that, nobody could believe it. We would put the worm on the long shank hook a certain way, thread the head and part of the body full on the hook to keep it from pulling off if nibbled, but the tease loop was more important, most important. Down the hook, where it bent around the bottom, a loop of worm would be left loose to wiggle.

The tease loop.

And then the rest of the worm on the remainder of the hook except for a half inch of tail to complement the tease loop.

The delivery was perhaps not important, as the lure or bait was perhaps not important, but we believed it to be and so worked the steel rods with our wrists, whipped them back and forth with six or eight feet of line, slammed them to get some action out of them, flipped the line forward and back and forward again to get it to land perfectly on the edge of the old weeds where the fish came to spawn.

But not like casting for northerns, this—not anything like it. When they are hitting—though the boys did not believe it—probably a bare hook would do as well as a baited one.

Sometimes they could be seen lying there and when the hook hit the water they would cut sideways, hit the hook so fast they would move the line to the side with a small hissing noise.

And fight. A two-pound sunfish, splashing gold up through the water, seemed to fight more than a five-pound northern or walleye. They would get the flat side toward the rod and run, planing off the flatness of their body, using it like a lever to fight the pull of the line, and it was never sure that they would be landed.

And one in three, perhaps only one in four, would wind up on the piece of wire used for a stringer to be brought to the pan.

Now fishermen fillet all fish as often as they can, cut the steaks off the side even when they are small, and fry them in deep fat with factory-prepared batter and factory-prepared grease and factory-prepared seasoning so that the fish all seem to be factory-processed. Like fish sticks.

But with the bulls, the water could be tasted in them, how they lived could be tasted, what they were. The fish were gutted and the egg sack saved. They were not filleted but scaled and the head cut off just in front of the hump of meat that came down to the fish's forehead.

This hump was the "sweet meat," along with northern tails, walleye cheeks, bullhead backs, and crawfish tails—all were special parts for the one who caught the fish to either eat as earned privilege or give away as a way to show respect, the way Inuit give away the best whale blubber.

The cooking varied, but always around a set method—frying.

The best was with bear grease. No grease, no lard nor shortening will ever equal strained bear grease for frying fish, pancakes, potatoes, or doughnuts. It is clear and stays liquid at room temperature and tastes of leaves and woods, and mixes with the taste of the fish, the water, the soft summer air.

The sunfish are fried whole in a large pan in a base of bear grease. Next to the fish the egg sack is cut open and the eggs are fried, and on the other side a pile of thinly sliced—thin as paper—raw potatoes are fried and the whole pan covered with a metal pie pan that is used as a plate so that while the food is cooking the steam carries heat and taste into the metal.

The cooking is finished when the skin lifts easily off the fish and is crunchy or when the smell has driven past where it can be tolerated or when hunger takes over.

Salt and pepper are sprinkled generously over the top, and it is eaten with the same knife used to clean the fish.

And all of this is better if done on a small fire made of dry poplar or hardwood on the shore near where the fish is caught along the edge, after snagging at the dam and spearing and casting for the big northerns, but still well before true summer fishing begins.

Sucker Hunting

When it was still cool at night but warming to hot in the days, when a jacket was too much during the day but not quite enough at night, there was a time for shooting suckers in the shallow lagoons.

Spawning was over for the suckers, the bottom feeders. They had run the ditches and streams that came in to the river and laid their eggs and in clouds of numbers they had been speared and shot and smoked and sold and eaten.

But they grew still in numbers, each female laying thousands and thousands of eggs until even the predators, the slashing northerns and schools of walleyes, couldn't keep them down, and the rivers and lakes teemed with them, huge blankets of them, gray backs touching gray backs so that when seen in the shallows it seemed they could be walked upon.

When the nights were cold and the days were

warm, sometimes, not always but sometimes, some of the suckers would come out of the rivers and lakes to lie in the shallow lagoons along the edge or in the backwater swamps where the water is rarely over one or two feet deep. Later in the summer the weeds and water lilies would grow to clog the lagoons, but early in the season the weeds weren't there and the suckers could be seen, would show like small dark logs just beneath the surface.

They were too fast to be speared and wouldn't take bait—and were not good to hook anyway as their mouths are too soft—but they were perfect to hunt with bows.

An old boat was used. None of us could afford a new one nor indeed afford anything but a free one so we would scrounge and dig and come up with an old bait boat made with cross-boards for a floor. Caution had to be used as the boards were simply nailed up from the bottom with common box nails, and if stood on directly their nails wouldn't hold and we would plummet straight through the bottom. By sitting on the seats and spreading our weight, we managed to make it all hold together, and paddles were fashioned out of old boards, carved and hacked with saws and hatchets.

Turns were taken. One person sat straddling the front of the boat, the bow with the arrow and fishing line ready, while the other sat in the stern paddling. The lagoons were entered slowly, carefully, and it was not a patched-up old bait boat with hacked paddles any longer but a slim canoe, a birchbark canoe gliding silently over the water from a time before, a time from books read and movies seen, a time before white men.

The fish seemed to think the boat was a log and moved slowly away as it approached, but even so, from a sitting position it was hard to hit them. The arrow almost invariably went high, and then came the laborious job of rewinding the line on the plastic water glass fastened to the bow, carefully laying it in rows so it would furl off evenly when the next shot was taken. If this were not done correctly sometimes the arrow would go out about twenty feet, the line would snarl and stop, and the arrow would snap back at the face of the shooter, point first; this could make for a lot of sudden activity in a boat that was about ready to fall apart, and almost all of the boys had a scar somewhere on their face from arrows hitting them.

Finally a position was found where the shooter kneels but raises up, and by shooting beneath the fish, almost as if there were another fish below the fish to aim at, it was possible to start making hits.

All of it was much slower than spearing or shooting them in a stream. If they were hit solidly near the back it was easy to boat them, but if the arrow passed through the main body, or worse, back by the tail, the fish ran and often cut back under the boat. Then it was necessary to manage the bow, the line—not stepping on the floorboards of the boat—a quiver full of homemade arrows, and the front paddle all at the same time.

It was, of course, impossible, and usually if the fish cut and ran under the boat, in the excitement somebody would step through the bottom of the boat and in moments it was full of water, floating just beneath the surface while the fight with the fish went on.

It is perhaps just as well that this type of fishing did not last long as most of the time seems to have been spent on the shore trying to get a fire going with wet matches to dry out clothes or feathers on arrows or hammering the boards back onto the bottom of the boat with a rock while the shoals and schools of suckers moved mockingly back and forth slowly across the lagoon just beneath the surface in the late spring sun.

The Ninth
Street Bridge

Real summer comes first when the lily pads and weeds along the edge of the river began to grow. It does not happen slowly, does not seem to occur gradually. One day the pads are not there and the weeds are all dry and brittle from winter and the next day the pads appear and the weeds are green and the summer water has life it did not have before.

The second sign of true summer is when the rock bass start biting down by the Ninth Street bridge.

It is thought that they start biting simply because the water temperature reaches a certain point—that would probably be the scientific answer. Or the weeds get a certain height, or the moon moves into a quadrant of the sky it must be in to make them hungry.

Whatever the reason, when they "come to start

biting," as the old people say, it marks the start of true summer fishing, and in this business of the Ninth Street bridge there are the first seeds of the real art.

It is not enough then nor now to simply bait a hook and lower it into the water and catch a fish and eat a fish. It has perhaps never been enough.

There are a hundred ways to do everything, but this principle seems truer of fishing by the Ninth Street bridge than of other things. Nothing is ignored in the search for perfection.

The rod, the kind of line, the hook—all are argued over, discussed to death.

"If the line is heavy you won't feel their mouth on the hook. . . ."

"Too much weight and they'll spit the bait. . . ."

"Wash your hands before you bait up or the stink will drive them back—nothing's as bad as man-stink. . . ."

It is likely that if a bent pin were hooked to a piece of baler twine and some bait wiped on the pin, the rock bass would bite, but nobody believes it, nobody wants to believe it.

It must take more.

And so the ritual begins. Any worm would work, but the worms from Halverson's backyard over near the corner of his clothesline back by his mother's favorite flower bed in that crumbly dirt that smells of sheep manure just after it has rained . . .

Those worms, those worms are the best.

They must then be carried right. Best is an old lard bucket with some of the dirt from where the worms were dug and a little water to keep the dirt moist plus just a dab of Steve's father's stale beer to "feed" the worms and kill the man-stink. (The beer is open for much argument—as to whether it works or not, what kind of beer is best, how stale it must be, and the best way to make it stale. Steve contends two days open is enough, but Wayne Kline swears that it takes longer, and Harvey Overton says none of it works unless you pee in the dirt on top of the beer, except that nobody likes to reach into the can for a worm if Harvey pees in it.)

Types of worms—large, fat, short, thin—also make for discussion and for a long time it was thought the sex of the worms mattered. This until it was found that worms are dual sexed; but none of it, none of the talk of baits or rigs or time of day or temperature or peeing or not peeing . . .

None of it compares to the complication of the actual fishing for the rock bass.

All fishing is complex, but this first true summer fishing seems the most important. Later in the summer mistakes can and will be made but this first time things must be perfect, and even the arrival at the bridge must be accomplished carefully.

Rods are carried across the handlebars, hooked in thumbs, and the bikes are old, fat-tired, hard to pedal, but are ridden carefully across the bridge and allowed to coast to a stop lest there be any undue noise. This in spite of the fact that trucks cross the bridge regularly and rattle the old timbers until dirt falls in.

Bikes are hidden. Chrome reflects light into the water so they are pulled well back and laid carefully, quietly on their sides and the edge of the bridge abutment approached.

The water moves past the rocks and concrete sidewall dark and murky, still looking muddy from the spring ditch runoff, coiling in tight eddies and swirls, making black holes where the year before or the year before that Roger Vetrum who was just fourteen and a doctor's only son and the papers said had everything to live for fell in and went under not three times but just the once. Just the one time and he didn't come up and never came up until they found him two days later a quarter of a mile downstream with mud in his eyes and his mouth, packed and dark and thick and bite marks where the turtles had been at him.

Along the abutment wall is where the rock bass are, nose up into the current, smelling for food.

The worm goes on the hook one of two ways. A small hook. Either the worm is threaded full on the hook, the metal shank and curve going through the body so it is hard to pull loose, or it is threaded on in loops with a tail left on to wiggle and tease in case the fish are not biting well.

A heavy sinker is used to fight the current, or a light one is used and the bait swung forward and dropped to drift back.

Willy read an article in *Field and Stream* about fishing. In the article the writer talked about "presenting the bait" to the fish, and only Willy read it, so for summer after summer in conversations about fishing he was an expert:

"Yes," he would say. "But that all depends on how you present the bait."

"No," he would say. "That depends on how you present the bait."

And while we laughed at him and made fun of him, we all secretly, in our hearts, thought he was right.

We all thought it mattered, and we thought of it that way—not as throwing the hook in the water or lowering it but as "presenting the bait."

It had to be "felt" into the fish's mouth, lowered along the wall high to let the current float it back, slowly lowering the line and the bait until it comes to a rock bass.

They don't bite hard, don't seem to bite at all. They come to the worm and in some way make a grating feeling on the bait, a rubbing feel/sound that somehow comes up the line and can be felt with a wet—not dry, but wet—finger and thumb just where the line goes into the reel.

Still it is not time to set the hook. Many times fish are lost because the hook is set too soon. Waiting is everything. The grating starts and then the fish will move away, come back, must be coaxed to bite. The bait must be raised, lowered, teased until the grating comes again and maybe even a third time, and then, when the bait is well in the fish's mouth, the hook can be set with an almost gentle but sudden raise of the rod tip.

The rock bass are seldom very large. A pound is rare. But they are very active and fight hard and often get loose from the hook, and, it was thought, learned from the experience to not bite again. At least we thought that until Duane Severson caught the same one twice, having dropped it by mistake the first time after landing it and recognizing a scar on its back from where a northern pike raked it.

The first one seems to take the longest, and some days they never bite and stringers go home empty. But when they start it can be hot and heavy for a time and usually enough are caught for a large meal for a family, and there is something special about the rock bass from the bridge. They are scaled but the heads left on for flavor and fried in clean fat, the fish rolled in a crushed-cracker batter, cooked until the skin just comes away from the meat and eaten the same day as they are caught, while everybody talks about catching them, bragging on this or laughing about something or another while chins get greasy and there is the knowledge that a whole summer is waiting to happen.

Lazy Fishing

After the rock-bass fishing down by the Ninth Street bridge there came the first "lazy fishing." There were times all summer when fishing would get lazy, but the first lazy fishing was a reaction to winter, to the length, the coldness, the depth of it.

When the first warm night came, a good solid warm day, perhaps even hot, followed by an early evening when the dog would barely raise his head when somebody walked by the hardware store—when it became that warm and soft something would pass between everybody and without really talking about things, without knowing how it happened, it was time for bullhead fishing.

Bullheads are northern catfish. Always fairly small—a pound and a half would be large—they were considered by the unintelligent to be rough fish, not worth eating. In fact in some small lakes and swamps they were poisoned out so "good" fish —walleyes—could be planted.

The poor knew better. The boys knew then why they would later come to be called such things as "fresh water lobster" and "fish filet mignon."

Because the state considered them to be rough fish—as they did perch and dogfish—there was virtually no limit and almost no control on the way they were fished.

The idea was to spend a whole night on a riverbank catching bullheads and dozing and then eat them with watermelon for dessert, but here too there was a form. A way that things must be done.

The place to fish was important, and many things entered into picking the right location. Since it was in the north there would be mosquitoes after dark—hordes of them—and so a small fire would have to be maintained with poplar leaves or grass thrown on the coals now and then to make smoke to drive them away. A place with dry firewood had to be found on the bank of the river where it left town and it had to be next to an eddy in the current so there would be a hole.

The bullheads like holes. Deep, dark, still holes.

They never bit during the day and only started about ten-thirty on a warm summer evening and after they started the biting was steady most of the night.

We did set lines and fished with rods as well. The

set lines we made by putting a hook and leader every four or five feet. Each hook was baited with worms or cut-up pieces of dead rotten chicks from the hatchery in town and the line thrown out with a rock to weight the end for distance. The set line would be left on the bottom where it fell for most of the night until most or all of the hooks were filled. (It is perhaps important to note that almost all of these methods are illegal in the north now.)

Along with the set we would work with rods with just one hook on the end. The advantage of a rod and reel was that we could cast past holes where there were only small bullheads and perhaps get larger ones, or a walleye—although walleyes were rare then in that river.

The bullheads bit like Huns. They would come in and swallow everything whole, taking the bait and hook and line well down their throats. They were very hard to get off the hook, requiring pliers, and were dangerous to work with because they had a spine in the top of their back and one on either side that had a mild poison on them and would hurt and swell when they got you. We quickly discovered a way to hold them, from the belly, with the palm against the belly and the thumb up in back of one spine and two fingers up alongside the other-side fin, and they could be worked off the hook and put on the cord stringer.

Biting ran in fits and starts. When they bit, they

bit hard and came fast, but when they stopped—sometimes for half an hour or more—it was time to nap or put a little wood on the fire and talk.

Talk. On our backs with the stars up above us, showing through wisps of smoke, the fire warming one side then another when we turned, talked and talked through the dark night.

Talked of girls.

Geraldine this and Sharon that, Shirley and Linda and Dianne—girls and more girls to talk about, dream about, sing about. This one to take to a movie, a scary movie, so scary that in the bad parts of the movie maybe she would throw her arms around . . . dreams and wishes, stories hoped to come true. We'd be walking along the sidewalk and she would be there and she would smile and her bicycle would be broken or her cat up a tree or, or, or . . . and she would be helped, saved, and she would be so grateful. . . . All night stories, dreams, prayers. When I get older and the pimples are gone and I have some money and my hair goes into a perfect flattop and I have the right clothes and I have a car, oh yes, a car like Harlan's '34 Dodge with the windshield that cranks up and I am popular, *then* she'll wish she'd gone out with me, been nicer to me, seen me.

In the middle of the night, finally, sleep comes and the fire dies and there is nothing until the first gray line comes up across on the east side of the river and the morning birds sing.

The set lines are pulled in and almost always there is a fish on each hook. They are added to the stringer, and if somebody thought ahead they remembered to bring the washtub and a wagon for hauling it. River water is put in the tub and all the bullheads are dumped in—upwards of a hundred of them—and taken home to clean. Depending on where they are to be cooked sometimes the fish are cleaned at the river, the guts let to slide with the current and feed other bullheads and snapping turtles that come up from the muddy bottom to strike at and grab the fish heads like something from a monster movie. That's if the cooking is at Wayne's house because his mother doesn't understand about things and doesn't want fish guts around even though we promised to turn them into the garden, which makes for good potatoes. But at other places there are cats and dogs to eat the guts and heads and the fish are taken home because some swear that the longer the heads are left on the better bullheads taste, although it is hard to see how they could taste better.

Hard to see how anything could taste better.

The fish are cleaned, the heads cut off and the meat washed in cool water and wiped with a towel to get the slime off the skin—they have no scales. The meat is a rich reddish color and when they are clean and wiped they are dipped in batter made from eggs and stale beer and then rolled in cracker crumbs mixed with pepper and fried in butter. They are done when the skin separates from the meat and the flakes of meat open like a book when they are pulled with a fork. There are some who fillet the bullheads but they are generally considered foolish because that takes away the skin, and the skin—crackling and tasting of butter—lends flavor to the meat and is itself good to eat.

You cannot catch enough of them. Maybe there aren't enough of them in the whole world. Jimmy Breshkov said once that it's impossible to keep up; that you could fish and catch bullheads and clean bullheads and fry bullheads and eat bullheads and by the time you buried the bones in the garden and went back to the river you would be hungry again and you could just keep going that way forever, catching and cleaning and eating them, but Jimmy is the same one who says ants never die because it's never been proven. He says nobody has ever seen an ant die of old age and Jimmy says that they're like the weeds in the Sargasso Sea that never die—one end shrivels off while the other end grows and they live forever, and he says there are plants that were alive when Columbus came through and so it must be true of ants as well.

But the bullheads *do* taste good, even if Jimmy is

wrong, and it is tempting always in the summer to try his theory and see if it works; see if it's possible to eat your way through a summer on bullheads and raw-fried potatoes and watermelon for dessert.

Walleye Fishing

These summers were long ago, so long ago that cigarettes were given to high school students by cigarette companies as a way to get them started and hooked; so long ago nobody had television and there were shows on the radio to listen to in the nights, back when portable radios cost an arm and a leg and took close to four pounds of batteries just to keep the tubes going for an hour and a half; and African-American people were kept from voting in the South and other places and did not have schools they could attend except for shacks. So very long ago that a teacher could—and often did—take a hardwood cane to a wiseass student (it made welts that lasted a week), and there were dress codes and curfews and tent revival meetings in the middle of town, and almost no drugs except what doctors prescribed and not a glimmer of the horror of AIDS, and all the streams and lakes in the north had not been fished out by greedy people.

There were truly large fish, many of them. Northern pike were considered not very good to eat because of the Y-bones down the side. They were eaten when caught but not favored and sometimes released. Once Duane Severson's father won a fishing trip up into Canada by bush-plane at a saloon raffle, and when Duane came back he told stories of not keeping any northern pike under twenty pounds and had the pictures to prove it. After that only really large northerns were kept and eaten, and even when Bill Wenstrom found a French recipe for baking northerns with the slime still on and they turned blue, people didn't eat them much if there were other fish available.

Walleyes were the cream of fish and while no-body yet called the big ones "lunkers," they were thought of that way.

The problem was that in the town the river had been pretty much fished out as far as big fish were concerned. So many people came down to the banks in the summer and worked there with rods and reels and set lines that respectable fish were virtually wiped out.

To catch big walleyes it was necessary to go out of town.

People who had money—we thought of them as rich people though they were probably only lower-middle class—had sleek wooden boats and trailers and would head out to the many lakes that surrounded the area, but we could never afford such luxury. Other people had canoes and would work the rivers and streams with them, but we could not afford even that until later.

There was the river.

It moved through town like a muddy huge worm, headed south below the power plant and dam and came from the north. South it went shallow, and so much farmland drained into it that the chemicals used by farmers for fertilizer and herbicide leached from the fields to the river and killed everything.

But north it came from the woods, was fed by a thousand small streams and swamps where fish could hatch and grow large and not be poisoned. North of town even a mile it was a different river, covered over with large trees that were so full of leaves they almost met overhead, making it a green tunnel filled with birdsongs and rustling brush so that it became impossible not to think of every Johnny Weissmuller Tarzan movie ever seen at Saturday matinees.

More than a mile north, two, four, six miles up the river, it was almost literally a wilderness that seemed untouched by humans. There were wolves there, big slab-sided gray wolves that sometimes showed in the brush on the banks, and bear that

worked the muddy sides of the river for clams, trying to stay ahead of the raccoons who hit the clams
and crayfish like Genghis Khan hit Asia.

And fish.

Here in the north part of the river, well north of
town, there were fish that had never seen a lure or a
line.

Really big fish.

There were holes along the banks, muddy swirls
that were ten, twelve feet deep, and down there in
the dark water, just above the muddy bottom waiting for food were walleyes, their yellow eyes glowing
in the murk.

Ten-, eleven-, twelve-pound walleyes.

The Cadillac of fish, according to an article
Wayne had read in *Sports Afield*.

The difficulty was getting to them.

A walleye-fishing expedition started with finding
a boat, and it was always difficult and sometimes
seemed impossible and always made the trip seem
more important than a fishing trip could ever be.

Willy's uncle had a sister-in-law who owned an
old beat-up cedar rowboat except that she didn't
have any oars, but Harlan's father worked with a
man who had a set of oars in his garage that he
never used, but Willy's uncle's sister-in-law needed
the boat that weekend because her nephew was
coming to visit so maybe we should ask the nephew
to come, except that he was a total jerkoff who had

never been fishing and was from the city and thought he was something else (cool) only he wasn't, but it didn't matter because Steve found an old wooden bait boat that only leaked a little and we could carve paddles out of two boards. . . .

And finding the boat was only the beginning. The initial walleye expedition also started so many side endeavors that it was difficult to remember the true reason for it all.

When a boat was located, and oars either carved or found, there was still the gear. What rods to take, the kinds of hooks, the line, the bait . . .

The bait.

Walleyes almost never rose to a lure—this was before the realistic minnow lures used now. They ate food, real food, and the two kinds of bait that worked the best were night crawlers (not just plain worms) and frogs.

Both difficult to get.

Night crawlers couldn't be dug because they were thought to be too deep. (Duane Severson used an extension cord plugged into a garage outlet and jammed two wires into the ground, trying to "shock" the night crawlers up; it might have worked, but Duane grabbed hold of the two wires just as his brother plugged the cord in and the experiment was called off rather suddenly.) But across the Ninth Street bridge in the woods near town there were old rotten logs, and during or just after a rain, if the logs were tipped quickly, the night crawlers were there and could be taken and stored in fresh dirt in a coffee can in the icebox—in those homes where this had not been tried before and the worms forgotten until a mother found them when they rotted. The smell of rotten worms in an icebox had a very dampening effect on family help for walleye expeditions.

Frogs were harder still.

There were almost no frogs in town. They had to be found in the river outside the city limits and stored to take in buckets on the trip. The difficulty lay in storing frogs. They couldn't be kept in the icebox—at least not since Wayne had tried it and his mother opened the icebox to have about thirty of them jump out at her.

Much research had been done on storing frogs. It took a week and more to gather them, and they had to be saved in a cool, damp place, and they could get out of almost any container.

Nobody was sure but it was thought that Wayne's dad or grandfather came up with the idea of the frog pit.

Whoever thought of it, frog pits sprang up all over the neighborhood. In back of every garage, the edges of gardens—anywhere and everywhere.

Two feet wide, three feet long, and at least three feet deep so the frogs couldn't jump out, the pits would be covered with a piece of tin and some loose grass or straw, and the earth would keep it cool and damp. They were perfect, and in the week before a walleye expedition everybody involved in the trip would be working along the river in both directions from town gathering frogs to put in the pit.

This was very important. Walleyes hit only fresh frogs and it might take four or five frogs to get a single fish. Fishing all night could take a person dozens of frogs and a three-day trip with three or four boys. . . .

It took a lot of frogs.

This meant that after the week of gathering there might be four, five hundred frogs in a pit. Sometimes more than one pit was used, but frequently mothers and fathers objected and had the pits filled in and so often all the frogs would be in one pit—a deep, squirming, slimy mass of frogs crawling over each other about a foot deep.

For those of us who liked frogs and used them for bait it was a lovely sight. For others it was not always so lovely and there is probably still talk of the time Dennis Hansen's mother was hanging clothes and stepped back from her clothesline directly into a pit full of frogs. This was long before women wore jeans or slacks very much and she had a dress on and sank with bare legs into a foot and a half of fresh frogs. The frogs immediately tried to use her legs to climb out and legend has it the sound she made—not a scream so much as a banshee wail—

cracked the leaded glass windows on St. Mary's Church nearly a block away.

Once the frogs and night crawlers were gathered, along with a can or two of regular worms in case no walleyes were found and it was necessary to fish for bullheads or panfish, it was time to turn to equipment.

It is probable that nothing is so important as equipment. Ever. Without equipment it is impossible to catch fish—the whole reason for the expedition would be lost without equipment.

Tackle boxes were not then the expensive and detailed, complete items they are now. None of us had anything new. Old rusty tackle boxes were found in the town dump with hinges gone and were fixed and sanded and painted carefully with names on them written with airplane model paint called dope for reasons that have never become clear. The tackle inside was usually limited to an extra roll of braided line, eight or nine snelled gut leaders (so called because they were then made with cat's guts, as were tennis rackets and violin and guitar strings), and a small metal container with a rotating window for hooks in case the snelled hooks broke or were lost. There was also a scaler made by screwing three bottle caps to a wooden handle and an old pair of needle-nose pliers for getting hooks out when they went too deep. A knife might also be included except that it was usually not in the tackle box but carried in a pocket or on a belt.

There was also "secret" equipment. No matter how close the boys were, everybody had at least one secret kind of lure or bait or idea to try for the really big one.

The lunker.

These secrets often cost money, and by selling papers in bars at night, waiting for the drunks to get juiced enough to hustle them for an extra quarter, or setting pins at the bowling alley or mowing yards or even caddying at the country club for the rich fat ones, it was possible to get enough money for special lures or a scent to squirt on bait or even a new reel to be hidden until just the right moment. Maybe to drop it in a conversation.

"Yeah, I was going to try working that deep place over by the bank with some of this new stuff on the bait. I sent for it through *Field and Stream.* . . ."

And a boy would pull out a small glass bottle of scent or maybe a new lure he'd been hiding, and even if it didn't work very well—and it seemed none of them did—it was still worth it just for the effect.

Finally it was all there.

Gear, more gear, equipment that had been cleaned and reels oiled with fine oil and knives sharpened and frogs and night crawlers put in buckets or cans, and everything had been checked and rechecked and rechecked again until it seemed things would be worn out from handling, and the boat was loaded, repacked, and reloaded, and on an early morning the expedition would at last be started.

Of course, it never worked like the plan.

Plans were always definite. Nights were spent sleeping over and making plans; talking until dawn about where it would be, how it would be, why it would be. Willy would actually draw pencil maps showing the whole river from where we started with detailed docks and houses along the way, every bend lined in accurately with possible holes where walleyes might be. There were drawings of these walleyes and other sketches of bullheads and northerns that looked like monsters, and the maps lost nothing because Willy had never been up the river on such an expedition before or maybe both eyes on a walleye seemed to be on the same side of the head. It was the effort that counted, and when a bend appeared on the real river that wasn't on the map or when the map showed a dock or house that wasn't really on the river nobody made fun of Willy. He kept a notebook and made corrections carefully, measuring distances with his eye and plotting possible good fishing locations as the boys rowed up the river.

Somehow all the boats we ever had were impossible to row easily, probably because they were old and heavy and always loaded way past good sense so there were only two or three inches of freeboard between the edge of the boat and the water. Three or four boys, what seemed tons of gear, a boat that was at best simply heavy, at worst waterlogged and just looking for an excuse to sink or capsize—all being powered by homemade paddles or old oars.

The trip was the hardest part.

Always when it started there was talk of getting far north.

"We've got to get up to the wild part," someone would say. "Where there aren't any people."

But miles take on new meaning when you are bucking the current; and there were some bends in the river where the current gained speed on the outside edge and it was quite possible to paddle or row as hard as we could and still the boat would sit in the same place, endlessly nosing into the current.

A trip that started by measuring miles on Willy's map ended with blisters and aching muscles not in miles but in effort, not in reaching wilderness but in reaching as far as one could reach before collapsing on the oars or paddles.

It was wild enough. Farms disappeared soon heading north, and within two miles the river closed in with thick brush and snarled wild grapevines that produced grapes so sour even Willy, who read a lot and called the grapes "Indian candy" and said Indians loved them, couldn't eat more than one or two without puckering and throwing up.

A place to stop was found, was fallen into, was delivered by God, at the end of the day just when dusk was coming, bringing the inevitable clouds of mosquitoes. It is important to note that this was not "camping." Camping was an art form in and of itself and had almost nothing to do with fishing.

Walleye expeditions were different from northern pike expeditions because walleyes always bit best in the night and northerns in the day and walleyes were for food more than sport, although there were those who said walleye meat wasn't all that good, was kind of flat, not as good as bullheads.

When a place was selected, a lean-to was erected and a fire made—the lean-to not to sleep in but for shelter in case it rained, and the fire not for cooking but to make smoke to keep mosquitoes away while the work at hand was performed, the hard work of fishing.

Frogs were hooked through the lower lip and left alive and moving, except by Willy, who stunned them by hitting them against a log before hooking them through the brain, which of course killed them. His argument was that they died anyway, drowned, but others pointed out that they moved for a while and during that time the big walleyes would go for them, and like many differences it was never resolved.

The frogs were hooked on a snelled leader, then a fairly heavy sinker was crimped on the line—this was prior to the rubber-twister sinkers and all that existed were the straight lead sinkers with fold-over tabs—about four feet above the hook, and the whole business was cast out into the middle of a hole or eddy or deep spot and left to sink on the bottom.

Walleyes were notoriously slow-mouthed and would come in the night, nose the frog, and work their mouth around it, and all of this must be felt with two fingers on the line; the different stages must be felt in the darkness with a low fire to make smoke and talking in whispers when talking at all. When the walleye first approached, when he opened his mouth and moved it over the frog, when he closed his mouth and his teeth grated gently on the line—everything about them had to be sensed through forty feet of braided nylon line and a gut leader. And when it was time, when the fish's mouth was over the frog, when all of that was *felt* to be correct, the hook could be set.

The hands lowered gently from the line to the cork handle of the rod, the handle was grasped slowly, carefully, and in a sudden swooping motion the rod raised up and back to drive the hook sticking through the frog's lip up and into the roof of the walleye's mouth, slamming past the barbs to hook him.

Many small ones are caught. The night is long, and though they stop biting well before dawn and many small ones are caught, nobody stops fishing until there is light and it is necessary to sleep, because there is always hope; there is always the soft prayer that in the bottom of the river, in the murk, there is a fish so large, a lunker of all lunkers waiting there, waiting to take your frog and your rod and whip them, twist them, and make you fight for your very place on shore.

That it never comes, that four-, five-pounders are there but the great gray-green monsters never come through the long night, or another long night, does not matter.

It is the trying that counts.

Northerns in
the Lily Pads

Day expeditions, when not working for walleyes but for northern pike, were similar to night-fishing trips except that more art was involved.

Fishing for walleyes took skill, but it was largely static, slow—sitting for hours in the smoke from the campfire, touching the line with the fingers, waiting for the grating of their teeth.

Northern pike were an entirely different matter.

There were three times to fish for northerns. The first was in the spring, right after the suckers ran, when the northerns took lures readily. The second time was in the middle of summer, and the last time was in the fall.

Fishing for northerns in the summer was like mounting a big-game hunt in Africa. It was very serious and focused on one thing and one thing only: using artificial lures to catch northern pike, preferably lures made by hand.

Nobody seemed to know when self-made lures started but everybody knew why—none of the boys could afford factory-made except for the red-and-white or black-and-white spoons known as daredevils. The daredevils worked well enough in the spring, and even through the summer, but usually worked only on smaller fish and were very hard to use in thick weeds or snags because they sank so quickly and the hooks were exposed so openly. Wooden plugs, made in the shape of a large minnow and painted to look like a fish or a red-and-white spark plug would float until the reeling-in phase of the cast started—when a lip would pull them under and set up the action. This meant the plug could be cast into a bad place next to a dead tree or snag—where large northerns liked to hunt for smaller fish—then pulled gently and slowly along the surface until it was clear and the fast-reeling retrieve could be started.

Plug-making went on all winter, a way to remember summer fishing when the snow was deep. Treble hooks and lip-spoons and eyelets could be ordered from sporting goods mail-order houses, and good plugs could be made for fifteen or twenty cents. They were carved of soft pine and sanded in the streamlined shape of a minnow or small fish and painted with airplane model dope, either with rib bones down the side and a dark back and green sides and bottom, or simply red and white—the front, or head, bright red and the rest of the body white.

Offbeat plugs first appeared one winter when a new boy moved in and had never fished for northerns. He painted realistic plugs like minnows, showing not just ribs but eyes and gill slits and mouths, like Flying Tiger aircraft. He also started the thought that the bigger the plug the bigger the fish, which culminated in Gene Tray making a plug nearly a foot long with five sets of treble hooks down the bottom and the end of a kitchen spoon for a diving lip under the chin. It looked good and everybody was anxious to try it, but it proved a disaster because his reel wasn't strong enough to take the weight of the plug during a cast. The first time he tried it the line fed out about ten feet and snarled in a horrendous backlash. It hung, the plug moving close to a hundred and fifty miles an hour, and hit the end of the line, bent the rod out and down and whipped up, around and back and buried three sets of hooks in the back of Gene's head. Four of the hooks went in well past the barb, driven in with tremendous force, some of them stuck deep in the skull itself, and the boys couldn't get them out even with fishing pliers. It was four miles back to town on bicycles, and Gene had to pedal all the way in with that wooden fish hanging out of the back of his head and that pretty much marked the end of trying with big plugs.

Moving out for northerns usually meant something of a military operation. In the summer the big northerns seemed to hole up where it was almost impossible to get to them. There were small lakes out around town where a boat wouldn't fit, but we could work to the shore through thick brush and we would bicycle out to them. Some lakes were ten miles away, and this was before thin-tired—what were called "English"—bicycles. We had huge steel beasts with fat balloon tires and shock-absorber front forks that weighed sixty or seventy pounds, and pedaling them ten miles on a gravel road, especially if the wind was wrong, could be a nightmare.

Northerns struck best early in the morning and in the evening, so we would leave when it was still dark, three-thirty or four in the morning, rods across the handlebars, hoping to reach the lake when it was still good for fishing.

They were very wary, so when we arrived at the lake each person would take a sector and work down to the shore through the brush carefully, quietly.

All these lakes were thick with lily pads. It was difficult to fish by casting over the pads because they would snag the plug and ruin the return. We would wade in, moving slowly, until the water was waist deep and we were at the edge of the pads, and then cast up and down the side of the pad bed, working the plug along the sides in smooth runs. The plugs would go deeper the harder they were reeled, and that gave some control of depth so the speed could be held to keep the plug two or three feet down, scooting and wobbling like an injured fish.

The northerns hid back in the pads, cruising there while they hunted panfish and minnows, and when the sun hit the lure they would come out like tanks, slashing and hitting so hard that if a boy wasn't ready they'd take the rod out of his hands.

Not huge—up to four, five pounds—these fish. But they fought like tigers and the plugs never hooked them that securely and often they would get off. And it seemed *always* the big ones would get away; always it was the one to tell about, the one to hold up hands about, the one to lie about that raised its ugly green head and slashed this way and that in the sunlight and the plug was gone, shaken loose to cartwheel away while the picture, the same picture as on the cover of every *Field and Stream* and *Outdoor Life, the* picture, burned itself into the eyes and mind forever.

Bobber Fishing

When a thing is done in the summer it is really never done; the fishing cycles, feeds back on itself and returns, so that the summer roars by and seems endless at the same time. When walleyes have been fished for it is time to do northerns, and then bullheads and northerns again and walleyes once more, around and around until it is not possible to say it is summer or just time to fish—until summer *is* fishing.

There is one other kind of fishing to make the summer—that is when we fished not to fish at all, but to be resting. It is perhaps not art then, but there is a kind of great joy in it.

Hole fishing.

Some of the boys sneered at it but there came a day each summer when somebody mentioned "bobber" fishing. It took courage to say it—we had become purists by then and some of us even filed the barbs off the hook to make the fish harder to catch —and the idea of throwing a line out with a red-and-white wooden bobber seemed to lack purpose.

But the truth was that fishing that way was too alluring not to do, and so we snorted and made fun and joked and teased but still went to fetch our cane poles and lines and bobbers and bicycled out of town to the best panfish hole.

A small hook set three feet below the bobber with a light sinker and a gob of worms brought up sunfish and bluegills by the hundreds, and it was mesmerizing watching the bobber as it hung there on the glass of the afternoon water. Then a nudge, another nudge, and suddenly it would go under as the fish ran, and a boy would pull up another sunfish flashing gold in the light—a calendar picture— swing the pole back and around and put the fish in a bucket of water to fry later.

Mostly to lie back, bobber fishing; mostly to soak up the sun and daydream. The fish are a minor part of it, a thing to justify lying back on a summer bank in deep grass, watching clouds make summer pictures in the sky and talking of what will come with life, with age, with time, and now and then to see the bobber sink and to pull in another fish.

"You know," Willy said one time when we were lying there. "All the thinking parts of living must be like bobber fishing. You lean back and your mind gets all flat and bam, you discover electricity. . . ."

Willy was the one who later found out about fly-fishing and started a craze that went for nearly half a summer. He read in an article in *Outdoor Life* about fly-fishing for trout on rivers in the Rocky Mountains and thought the boys should try it. The problem was there were no mountains and no streams and no trout. But Willy wasn't one to see the problems, only the solutions, and he rigged up a kind of fly rod with a cane pole.

Nobody had flies so he made some with hair cut from his mother's poodle. She found out about it even though he took it from underneath where it didn't really show and that was nearly the end of fly-fishing, and in a way it was just as well. Once all the boys got into it the poodle wouldn't have had enough hair anyway. But about then Jimmy found an old stuffed deer head in the attic of his garage and that gave everybody enough hair.

The hair was crudely tied to small hooks with wrapped, braided fishing line, painted with airplane model dope, and then we had to find some fish.

Of course not all fish will rise to a fly and it would be many years before trout were stocked, but Willy tried along the lily pads one day when we were bobber fishing, and the sunfish and bluegills rose.

That's all it took, and for the rest of that summer fly-fishing was all the rage. None of us had fly rods or the right kinds of line or reels but that didn't stop

anybody. We made flies with anything we could get
—the deer hair, tinfoil, bits of old diapers, string,
even bare hooks painted gold with dope.

The fish rose to them all. They would hide back
under the lily pads from the northerns who cruised
the outside edges looking for food, and when the fly
plunked down between two pads they couldn't re-
sist and came barreling out to hit it.

That was the same summer that Wayne found an
old pair of rubber swim goggles and we took turns
swimming around the lily pads watching the sunfish
and northerns until Wayne saw a musky that ran
maybe twenty or twenty-five pounds but looked like
it weighed a hundred. He wouldn't go in again. Said
it looked too mean, like it could take something
right off you, and his fear was infectious enough
that it scared all the boys and that stopped the diving.

Fishing Madness

Some fished for fun and some for something else and a few were driven crazy by it, so that they became complete purists. As summer ended the true addicts, the ones who even when young knew they would be fishing for the rest of their lives, restlessly moving along a bank or working out of a boat—as the last weeks in summer came, those who thought of only fishing prepared for the kind that almost always ended in failure.

Musky fishing.

Muskies are a cousin to northern pike only usually much larger. Thirty- and forty-pounders were not uncommon then (although they are rare now) and they fought hard enough that they sometimes tired the fisherman before they could be brought to shore or alongside the boat.

Everything about them was myth. Size, the way they fought, what kind of lure they struck—all rumors, sayings, dreams. It was said that it took a thousand casts to get a strike, ten strikes to get a fish, and a hundred strikes to get a big one. Many (this author included) have fished for muskies with lures for years, all their lives, and never landed one, and so everything known about them comes from somebody else. Somebody's cousin who knew a friend who met somebody who was using a large silver spoon for a lure and had a thirty-, forty-, fifty-pound musky take his rod completely away, over the side and gone and done, though he was strong and held hard.

The method was simple. A good reel, stout line (thirty- to forty-pound test), a steel leader (muskies' teeth cut through line like butter) and a good lure. The lures were very expensive and we could not afford more than one, so care had to be taken to get the right one. Many said the best lure was a large silver or golden spoon with red-jewel bug-eyes and everybody knew somebody who knew somebody who had had a strike on this bug-eye. The problem was that they were steel and weighed close to a quarter pound, and when they hit the water you had to start reeling as fast as you could because they sank like a stone and would catch every snag there was on the bottom. Another lure that worked well, or that was said to work well, looked like a baby duck with big treble hooks hanging out its bottom (muskies loved to eat baby ducks and loons) and little orange legs that rotated when the lure was pulled across the water. The advantage here was that the lure floated and was controllable and wasn't so easily lost, but it cost so much that many either went with the bug-eye or tried making their own baby ducks. The procedure was the same in any event. Cast out as far as possible and reel in as fast as the crank will turn.

Then do it again.

And again.

And again.

Alone in the hot sun on the bank, over and over until your arm seems about to come off, until it is agony to cast even one more time.

Then again.

And again.

Musky fishing, along with fall fishing, is the purest form—not just of fishing but of torture. To stand for hours, days, casting and recasting and never a hit, never a strike, never a follow-up.

It's madness.

And everyone who tries it must go back; though they live forever, they always must go back and try it one more time. There's always the chance that on the next cast, the very next cast, a green-backed submarine will come up from the dark weeds and the line will hiss out so fast it burns your thumb and it's—all—right—there, on the next cast.

Madness.

• • •

Finally summer is done, not suddenly, but with a last flurry of fishing, a last time at the hole with cane poles, a last night of bullheads, a last try at the walleyes or working the rock bass down by the Ninth Street bridge. A day comes when leaves start to dry and curl up and there is a coolness in the air. Fishing begins to end.

Except for some.

With the first frost, and first ice on the edge of the river, the sane ones quit. The ones with lives, with families, oil their reels and wrap them in soft rags for the next year; prepare themselves for winter fishing.

But there are a few diehards who know the secret that the old-timers talked about sometimes sitting around the smokehouses eating salty smoked fish and drinking beer cooled in a tub of water.

Just as the ice comes, just with the first hard freeze and when the wind starts bringing storms down from Canada and there is new snow starting to show and stay—just then, when all the boats are put away and motors drained of oil and people are settling in for winter . . .

Just then the big northerns come out to play.

It is a hard time to fish. Nothing goes right. It is best to use lures and work where a river runs into a lake or where a stream runs into a river, working the lure across the opening. The lure must move across the current at an angle and seem to be sliding sideways while it moves, slipping along with a jerk and wobble. Again, a bug-eyed spoon seemed to work best, but most couldn't afford them and so used homemade plugs. Brightness seemed to be most effective and a flash-white plug with a red head, reeled in as fast as a hand could turn a reel handle to make it run deep and keep it wobbling and jerking as rapidly as possible, could be made almost irresistible.

Each cast was torture. The weather had to be cold for the big ones to come and that made it almost impossible to fish. Bundled in coats, we would stand in ice mixed with water in old five-buckle overshoes, and every time the line came in it had to be squeezed between thumb and forefinger to compress the water out of it or it would freeze on the reel in a solid lump. This meant that water was constantly dripping down the hand and freezing on the fingers and in the cuff along the wrist. Feet wet, frozen, water freezing all down the front, snow falling and winter coming, and one more cast.

When they hit, and they hit often, it was with the complete savagery of desperation. Either from instinct or knowledge, the fish knew winter was coming, and knew that they had to eat and build up fat for the lean times; and the old ones, the big ones, knew it better than the small young ones. So almost every cast brought a strike from a large fish, and the strikes came from the side or bottom—it was hard to tell—and seemed to drive the lure sideways or up as if it were getting hit by a train.

Soon the fingers were numb, and the hands, and feet, and the pain came, and everything inside said quit now, quit, the year is done, summer fishing is done.

But something held, something pulled, and it seemed always there was one more cast, and one more strike and one more big northern until it was the last day, dark on the last day, snow falling heavily and people getting ready for Thanksgiving and still a part says it isn't over, summer can't be over, and still one more cast. . . .

Fishhouse
Dreams

S ometimes cold weather came long before snow and there was enough time for the rivers and lakes to freeze without snow accumulating on the ice. This period would not last long but when it came, as soon as the ice was thick enough to hold weight, we would skate on it.

Not to just skate or play hockey but to go and see country. The rivers became ice highways that led to lakes, small frozen streams, openings into the wilderness that usually lasted only a week or so and demanded exploration. Skates allowed speed and we flew through the early winter, and while most of these explorations were for hunting, now and then they led to fishing.

Light brought the fish to the surface, or as close to the surface as they could get, rubbing their backs along the ice, and skating above them we could see them. Somebody thought of chopping a hole through the ice—usually only a couple of inches deep—and trying to "herd" the fish into the opening where they could be netted, and after trying for hours we finally caught a northern in a dip net, and after that we always tried to do this when the ice froze before the snow came.

When the ice finally became thick enough to hold serious weight—usually by early December—the ice fishing season would start. There were two methods. Nobody could afford fancy augers so usually an old axe was used to cut a hole in the ice and we fashioned homemade tip-ups to use for rigs. A tip-up was just a stick across the hole and another across that, the two bolted or tied in the middle to make a cross. From the end of one, a line was tied with a sinker and hook, and it hung about six or eight feet below the ice with a piece of raw chicken or a silver pickled minnow (if they could be afforded) bought from the bait shop.

Then everybody went to shore and gathered firewood enough for a bonfire, which was made on the ice not too far from the hole. The boys would stand by the fire watching the tip-ups and waiting for a fish to come along.

When a fish took the bait—usually a panfish, crappie or bluegill—the one stick would flip up in the air and the fish could be jerked up. It was simple and not really fishing so much as just taking fish.

The other method involved using a fishhouse. In the winter people would put small houses on all the

lakes and rivers, huts really. In the floor of each house a hole was cut and a similar hole cut in the ice beneath the fishhouse. Inside the fishhouse it was kept dark, and hours could be spent watching down in the green hole, jigging a lure up and down to draw northerns in where they could be speared with a ten-tined, foot-wide spear.

There were many dreams in fishhouses. Dreams of summer, dreams of ends and beginnings and of how it all started when the car fell through the ice and would all start again next spring. A little stove burned sticks and shavings and kept the fishhouse toasty and comfortable, and all that had to be done was to sit and stare down in the emerald-green hole, watching the lure and waiting for the northerns. When they came it was suddenly, impossibly quick. One second there was the lure, the next a huge fish either nosing it or taking it—slash, and it was there —and then the lunge with the spear, trying to put the tines across his back and missing often. So fast, so lightning-fast that they could move away while the spear was on the way down.

And then the green again; the deep green from the water coming up through the hole while we waited, waited for another fish, waited for deep winter, waited for the end of the white blanket that covered all things, waited for the end of cold, blue cold.

Waited for summer and fishing to start again.

Camping

Running the River

There came a time in the almost exact center of the summer when, as impossible as it was to believe, fishing paled. Not permanently. Not even for long enough to measure.

"Let's go down to the Ninth Street bridge and catch some rock bass," somebody suggests, and everybody shakes his head.

"We did that yesterday."

"We could go out for frogs. There are bullfrogs just thick out by Peterson's slough. . . ."

"We've got all the frogs we need."

"Well then, what?"

A pause, a breath, because this cannot be wasted —this time, this only time when the sun is still there and the sky is still there and the soft days and softer nights are still there, and if there is no fishing and it is still too fine and wonderful to stay inside, to stay in town, well then, what?

"Let's go camping."

And there it is. How could nobody think of it each summer until this moment, when it is so logical, so right? And suddenly there is nothing else, no other thing in the whole world than to go camping.

But first, as with hunting and fishing, first there is the planning.

Where to go?

Hours, days, spent on just where to go when always, never changing, there is the river. It is the highway to all things, the river, winding muddy and slow and inviting, a road to all the adventure in all the books. Books by Twain and London and Burroughs, books about rivers and of rivers and in rivers, read and reread, dreamed and redreamed, and so there is never really any choice, and talk goes on until somebody at last says it:

"Let's run up the river."

And then more planning. How to get a boat when there is no boat, this time not even one to borrow from Wayne's aunt, nothing but the old bait boat with the boards nailed across which never works but is all there is, and it is dragged up on the shore at the edge of the swamp and all the boards renailed and bits of rag tucked in the cracks with a screwdriver.

"Don't worry," somebody says. "It'll leak at first until the wood swells and then she'll tighten right up."

"Hell," another one says. "Columbus crossed in a boat worse than this. We're just running the river for a couple of days. It'll work fine."

And everybody nods and nobody asks how four boys and gear are going to fit into the old flat-bottom bait boat.

We just know; all will fit in and the wood will swell and the leaks will stop and there is that . . . that thing, that smell, that fresh adventure calling from up the river so it will all work out.

Gear is selected. No fishing this time, no hunting, only to go and lie by the river with a fire at night and look up at the stars and talk about what will be, could be, should be.

Gear for comfort.

An old army surplus pup tent and a piece of canvas for a tarp because it always rains. The tent for two men will sleep three boys easily, four if the tarp is used.

Blankets. This was before sleeping bags. Blankets and an old quilt are wrapped and rolled in the tents but they will not be needed because even in rain, even in clouds and wind and rain, it is still summer and the nights are hot and damp, and a single blanket works to help keep the mosquitoes off when the fire dies down and the smoke is gone.

But still blankets, two, three for each boy, more blankets than can fit in the boat, and the largest part of planning hasn't yet begun.

Food is next. Hunting and fishing take "fixin's," flour to cook fish or a pan to cook meat, but all food is carried on camping. Enough food for thirty days is carried. Everything that has ever been wanted and can be afforded is taken except by Bill, whose father is a grocer. He has to bring all past-dated fruit and vegetables because his father will not give him things that can be sold.

Wayne brings all the cans of Spam he can find because he loves Spam, cooked, raw, sliced, in chunks, Spam, and Kool-Aid made from spring water and cupfuls, not spoonfuls, but cups of sugar.

Marshmallows and hot dogs and a stream of cans of pork-and-beans and soft tasteless white bread and jars of peanut butter that doesn't stick to the roof of your mouth and some that does and grape jelly in small jars with cartoons on the sides and more marshmallows and more beans and cans of corned beef hash and large potatoes and tinfoil to bake them in the fire until they are burned black and taste like charcoal and bags of cookies, Oreos and the kind that are filled with marshmallow, and there are never enough in the box, and still more hot dogs and one, one jar of pickles and two more loaves of bread and one last bag of marshmallows and two pounds of raw hamburger to fry in an old pan, all in a pile on the bank next to the boat.

And that was just for one boy.

Food for the masses, food for towns, was stacked

on the bank next to the bait boat. Food until it couldn't possibly all fit in the boat, stacked and waiting and still one boy not there, still to come one more pile and at the last, disaster.

Every last thing is thought of and no matter how many times the camping is done there is always some last-minute disaster that seems to come to ruin everything.

When Bruce comes to the boat, all his food in sacks on his bicycle, there is another boy with him helping to push the bicycle, a last-minute boy.

"This is Gilson," Bruce says. "He's an exchange student from South America. They sent him up early so he could work on his English." And then the curse, the words that nobody wants to hear, the doom words. "Pa says we've got to take him with us."

Five boys then. Gilson, it turns out, cannot speak more than forty or so words in English, many of them almost wonderfully foul and almost all of them used completely in the wrong context.

"I am damn," he says, smiling at us. "Is the boat screw?"

Nobody wants to take him.

"He'll be fine," Bruce says, trying to put the best light on it. "All he does is smile and give everybody the finger. . . ."

And since Bruce is one of the all-for-one and one-for-all summer gang that camps and fishes, since that is the way it is, we must take Gilson or leave Bruce, and it is unthinkable to leave Bruce.

With gear and paddles and five boys, when the boat is pushed away from shore and an attempt is made to paddle it upstream, it is impossible, and only two inches of freeboard exist between floating and sinking and the wood hasn't swelled yet so it leaks.

"Son of a bitch," Gilson says. "Water more boat. . . ."

Command decisions are made, all mistakes. As heavy as the boat rides it will not paddle upstream, hangs like a half-sunken log in the current, and Wayne says what everybody is thinking.

"We'll float downstream—it'll be easier to paddle her back light."

It makes no logical sense. Except for some of the food being gone (eaten), all the other gear and all the boys would still be with the boat, and it wouldn't be any lighter. But it somehow sounds sensible and the boat is moved into middle current and catches the river and slides off out of town.

Hot morning sun beating down. Steering the boat now and then with an idle push of the homemade paddles. Drifting on through town, the boat really just on the verge of sinking, portaging the short walk around the dam and reloading and finding the current again.

The boat moves deceptively fast. The current

seems sluggish, more so as the morning turns to noon and the day-heat comes, but as slow as it seems, the river is moving fast, faster than a quick walk, carrying boys and food away from town.

Some notice. Wayne has science knowledge and uses his fingers as a gauge to measure progress against dead trees on the bank and says, "You know, we're moving right along" and "I think we're hitting at least four point six miles an hour" and "I've been calculating, and if we're moving at four point six miles an hour and we've been drifting for four hours, we've come roughly eighteen point four miles. . . ."

But nobody listens.

The day is warm, the sky is completely open and blue; and in broken English, almost crippled English, and awe-inspiring gestures Gilson has revealed that he is almost a year older than anybody in the boat, lives in Rio de Janeiro, that there are prostitutes there and that he has availed himself of them not once but—holding up his fingers—four times.

Telling all this, using the limited language and his hands, takes considerable time, and the audience —at an age when hormones run wild—is raptly attentive and does not notice the current or the distance traveled. There are many questions of a technical nature and each answer takes Gilson considerable time.

Mile floats past aimless mile while Gilson struggles to describe how it was to Know Things, and when disaster comes it happens so fast and with such finality that it almost isn't accepted.

Gilson's hand is in the air—something to do with female anatomy—he is struggling for a word, the perfect word, when there is a slight bumping sound beneath the hull and without further warning a short limb from a sunken snag jams through the boards and rips the entire bottom out of the boat.

A half-second hangs, Gilson's hand in the air, all eyes on the hand, the boat bottom gone; half a second, and then everything, everything goes under.

The boat, already waterlogged, sinks like a stone and all the gear with it. There is time for nothing but survival. It has happened so fast Gilson's hand is still in the air when he goes under, his eyes wide. Somebody has time for half of a foul word and then five boys are in and under the muddy water.

Three heads come up sputtering, then four, and finally Gilson, who—it turns out—cannot, could not swim but has learned quickly how to do a cross between a paddlewheel riverboat and a thrashing dog and comes up in a spray of muddy water and eloquent Latin-based curses.

"All right," Wayne starts, treading water, "whose job was it to check the bottom boards?"

But again, nobody listens, and Gilson—having had his fill of river water—wheels and aims for shore, leaving a rooster tail like a speedboat.

The problem is that there isn't a shore. The river has been winding deeper and deeper into thick forest, really northern jungle, and the undergrowth grows to the edge of the river and out, so thick it is hard to push an arm through it, let alone a body, so thick it prevents Gilson from leaving the river, from doing anything but hang on a limb staring at the muddy water around him whispering softly: "Snakes? Is snakes here?"

Wayne finds a hole away from the bank, two feet across, high enough to crawl where a beaver has dragged a log down the bank, and he pulls himself up out of the water and disappears into the green wall as if he's been swallowed.

"Come on." His voice is muffled, within a few feet, and it's almost impossible to hear him. "It's nice in here. . . ."

He has lied. We all follow him, slipping up from the water in the mud of the river's side and into the greenness, the thick green of the forest, but he has lied to us.

It is not "nice."

As soon as we are out of the sun and into green —so thick it wraps us, so close and cloying that Bruce hisses, "It's like being in a jar of lime Kool-Aid"—as soon as we clear the direct light of the sun, the mosquitoes find us.

Hordes, clouds, a mass so thick they cover all skin, sting the eyes, every inch they can reach, mil-

lions of them come at us so terribly that Gilson—
who is almost totally urban and knows nothing of
forests except for stories of the Brazilian rain forests
and headhunters and snakes—Gilson goes mad with
the mosquitoes, screaming and trying to run away
from them. He is quickly tangled in hazel brush and
wild grapevines, fights free and scrambles back
down the tunnel to the river, where he sits sub-
merged up to his neck refusing to come back out.

"We need a fire," Wayne says. "To make some
smoke to drive them away."

"All the matches were in the boat. . . ."

"Not all. I have some in my waterproof pocket
container, along with salt and pepper."

"You would. . . ."

But nobody complains when he scrapes some
kindling together and uses one of the matches to
start a small smudge fire that, miraculously, does
work; the whiffs of smoke drive the mosquitoes
away, and after convincing Gilson to leave the river
and come under the protection of the smoke, there
is time to consider the predicament.

"How far," somebody asks, "do you think we
came down the river?"

"Twenty-four point seven miles." Wayne coughs.

Everybody stares at Wayne.

"How do you know that?"

"Well if we were doing four point six miles an
hour and we traveled . . ."

"All right, all right."

"Of course the river winds a lot. In a straight shot we're probably fourteen or fifteen miles from town. If we walk at an average of three miles an hour it's going to be five, six hours. But the woods are so thick I don't think we'll make two, maybe a mile and a half an hour. Say twelve, sixteen hours of walking."

Everybody has been silent except Gilson, who is looking for snakes again and does not seem to understand that there are no poisonous snakes in the north woods.

"What if we cut straight out?" Bruce points away from the river. "What's out there?"

"Ten, twelve miles of woods and then the highway. God knows how many swamps. We're better off walking straight back to town. . . ."

"I'm hungry." Lloyd has been silent all this time. Like Gilson he did not know how to swim and learned on the way down with the boat and has been quiet since he came to shore. Until now. "I could eat rotten fish. . . ."

"All the food went down with the boat."

"I know. I'm still hungry."

"Keep it to yourself."

"I'm *still* hungry." As if he thought it would go away by talking about it.

Argument followed discussion followed argument, standing in the smoke from leaves thrown on the fire, and nothing is agreed on by all people. Two think it would be wise to strike for the highway and two think it would be smartest to follow the river, with Gilson dissenting in ignorance. It is decided to vote and to give Gilson a chance to vote as well, though he has almost no idea of what is happening, and explaining it to him—as explaining that there are no poisonous snakes or jaguars in northern Minnesota—borders on the absurd. Any sound, the crack of a twig on the fire, Lloyd farting—any little sound and Gilson jumps a foot in the air and heads back for the river.

Finally a vote is cast, and with much yelling and gesticulating Gilson casts his vote for following the river.

"Hell," Lloyd says, "he thinks he's voting for a ride to town."

"It don't matter." Wayne shakes his head. "Elections are elections. The vote is done. We follow the river."

It was much easier to say than to do. There are game trails, but they wind like snakes and go in no consistent direction for more than ten or fifteen yards, and trying to move off the trails is like hitting a wall. Vines and thorns catch at clothing and skin, hold, impale, and soon everybody is cut and bleeding.

"How far do you think we've come?" Lloyd asks after half an hour.

"Maybe fifty yards. I can still see the smoke from our smudge hanging in the trees back there."

"How fast does that make us?"

"We'll get home," Wayne says, looking up at the sky—for what reason nobody can define except that it gives him an air of knowledge—and calculating, "day after tomorrow, late in the day. If we keep moving at this speed and don't stop to rest, or sleep or eat."

"Eat, hell. There ain't nothing to eat."

"Snakes?"

"No, Gilson. No snakes. None. Not any snakes."

It is at this precise instant Gilson steps on a snake. It is a garter snake, completely harmless except to frogs, about two feet long and just trying to cross the trail. Gilson steps on the tail and the snake responds by biting at his ankle. Garter snakes have no teeth and the response is purely automatic and cannot hurt, but Gilson looks down just as the snake is striking and there is nothing in the world that can stop him.

He makes a sound like a muffled steam whistle and leaves. Simply leaves. One instant Gilson is there, in the middle of the group, and the next he is gone, vanished, having gone straight ahead in a shower of falling brush and ripping vines.

"Well," Wayne says, watching him go, "he's heading in the right direction and leaving a good trail. Let's follow him."

Gilson makes almost a hundred and fifty yards before wearing down, and his trail makes for easy walking until we come up on where he has stopped.

"Morte," he says, and we would not know what he means except that Wayne had seen the word in a comic book about Cisco Kid.

"It's death," he says. "He thinks he's dying."

"He sure made it easy getting here, breaking trail for us." Lloyd looks back at the distance covered. "Did anybody think to pick up the snake? We could use it again. Kind of keep him going with it."

But nobody has thought of the snake, and after a moment Gilson is dragged to his feet—Wayne says he is confessing his sins by this time and wants to listen in case there's anything good about the prostitutes—and we start again, weaving through the brush.

It is nightmarish going. Slow enough so the mosquitoes can follow easily, and the undergrowth and trees keep away any chance of breeze to force them down.

We are savaged by them. At first it helps to brush them away, but there are too many and at last we can only slog along, swollen with bites, thirsty and hungry, until near dark.

"Now," Lloyd says, "I'm *really* hungry."

"We can't travel in the dark," Wayne says. "Not without seeing the stars."

Everybody gathers wood for a fire. Everybody

except Gilson, who has cleared a spot with his foot and is standing in the middle looking for snakes, and soon a fire is going and the mosquitoes are once again at bay. Working through the day has dried our clothing, and the fire raises spirits and Lloyd has amassed enough wood to burn for several nights, let alone one, and talk starts up about Gilson and the prostitutes and it is some time before anybody notices that Wayne is gone.

"Where did he go?" Lloyd asks.

"Did anybody hear a scream or anything?"

"Snakes?"

"Wayne!"

There is nothing, no sound. Somebody throws more wood on the fire, heaps it until the flames go up fifteen feet, and we search in the light from the fire but there is no sign.

"What could have happened?" Lloyd moves closer to the fire. "He was right here and then he just disappeared. . . . God, you don't suppose a bear took him, do you?"

"I don't think a bear would *want* him."

"We'd have heard something. A yell, something. . . ."

"We should look for him."

"In the dark?"

Wayne was gone. More yelling was done, even Gilson forgetting the "jungle" long enough to add his voice but there was no answer and it was decided

—after much argument—to wait until daylight to look for him.

"Maybe he went back to the river, fell in and drowned . . ."

All knew stories of boys who drowned in the river. Never girls, always boys going down in the murky water and not coming up because the temperature was so low it kept the bodies from generating gas to make them float. Put just that way. "The bodies don't generate gas to make them float. . . ."

But looking in the dark at the river would aid nothing, and others might drop in and drown and so, finally, more wood and still more wood is put on the fire and everybody lies strangely quiet, looking at the flames, until Lloyd starts:

"You know, I liked Wayne. Always have. . . ."

"Yeah, he's all right. A little too full of numbers and stuff but not bad. . . ."

And more until an hour has passed, everybody thinking Wayne has dropped in the river and getting sadder and sadder until there is a sound, a crackling in the brush, and Wayne comes into the firelight.

Everybody is startled and jumps, including Gilson, who heads for the river again in the dark and has to be tackled and dragged back.

"What are you carrying?"

Wayne is holding a large object in his hands and when he gets into the light Lloyd identifies it.

"A shovel?"

He has an old scoop shovel, the handle long rotted away, and it is filled with eggs.

"Eggs?" Lloyd says. "Where'd you get eggs?"

"There's a farm. Not half a mile away." He is still breathing hard from trotting. "I heard a chicken squawk earlier and thought I should go investigate it. The people were gone but I found the chicken coop and the eggs and this old shovel to cook in. Oh, there's a driveway. We can walk out tomorrow, get to the highway and hitch home. . . ."

Three dozen eggs, mixed brown and white, and eager hands cracked them in the shovel until they were a large puddle. Then onto the fire, the shovel full of eggs, stirred with a stick as they fry, burn, smoke, smell, bits of rust and dirt and God knows what else from the shovel until the eggs are done and then—with great flair—Wayne produces his waterproof salt and pepper shakers to season the eggs.

Then to eat them. A full day without food and the eggs with salt and pepper and hot, eaten with fingers, a fair share each. Not enough to fill, and dry without grease, but, God, so delicious and wonderful that once Lloyd—who likes food more than anything—turns so his face catches the light and it can be seen he is crying, chewing eggs and crying softly.

Then around the fire, lying down, the smoke and heat keeping the insects away, the forest a black wall to the edge of the light, we lie, dozing in and out, while Gilson—content, safe by the flames— picks up the story of the prostitutes exactly where he left off when the boat sank beneath him. And just before sleep, just before the last moment of the day goes under, Bill says:

"Hell, this is fun. Where we going to sink next year?"

And everybody nods, agrees, and tries to remember if last year's camping was as good as this year's. . . .

Hunting

Fool Hens

Hunting always began with excitement. Not ordinary breath-catching, first-girl, first-love, first-success, first-child, first-time excitement.

Nothing that superficial.

The kind of hunting almost didn't matter—just the act. To hunt.

It always started in the fall.

Summer was fishing, and then school—God, school, the great bother of it all—trying, trying to fit in, trying to be part of, trying to understand, trying to learn, trying to be accepted, trying to look right, trying to act right, feel right, say right, do right, be right.

And failing at all, most, all. Grades bad, clothes wrong, never any money, hair that never worked into a flattop or a ducktail—just impossible. To wear wrong clothes and be from the wrong place in town and have the wrong parents and think the wrong thoughts and to feel, to suspect, to know that everyone is looking, pointing, laughing. School.

All summer, fishing, camping, looking for the best places and largest fish. Talking of dreams and some hopes and large brags, and when school started the same boys came with the same problems. School became not a place to learn so much as a way to meet, to talk. In the halls between classes, sometimes in class with notes passed back and forth, drawings, maps, all aimed at one point—hunting. To plan hunting. Study hall was perfect. Whole notebooks could be moved back and forth while the football coach who monitored study hall stared out the window or at the ceiling or dozed. Physical education was the same. Everybody had to run but it was easy to hide in back of the bleachers outside or in the gym and talk, sometimes sneaking drags on forbidden cigarettes while plans were made.

Planning was perhaps the most important thing, a constant. During school but also afterwards on the walk home or at night while setting pins in the bowling alley or selling newspapers or hiding from parents—always there was planning.

The plans varied with the kind of hunting contemplated but were still everything; where to go, what kind of equipment, expected game, how to find the game, how to bring the game home, how to prepare the game; and it was always "the game," ever since one boy read the phrase in *Sports Afield*.

Plans allowed the excitement to live, to continue, even when it wasn't possible to hunt, but even planning didn't change one other constant.

In the fall, toward the end of September, the first hunt was always grouse.

Ruffed grouse, sometimes erroneously called partridge, also fool hens, spruce hens—it didn't matter.

They were the first.

The state picked a day when grouse season opened, a day late in September when it was legal to go into the woods after them, but it didn't ever mean anything.

There was another day that counted more.

Summer died hard, hanging on with hot muggy days that never seemed to end, hung on well into September. Gardens came into full ripening, and the boys would "go gardening"—work around town in late August nights from one backyard garden to the next with a salt shaker to use on vine-ripened tomatoes eaten fresh from the plants, tomatoes that tasted of summer and earth and dust and night all at once, tomatoes to bite hard and make the juice run down the chin, to eat until it was hard to walk.

Summer died hard, with high-moon nights in the playgrounds, swinging and teasing Sharon or Darlene or Mary, pushing them higher and higher on the swings until they shone in the moon all pigtails and legs and teeth and laughter.

Summer died hard, going to the fair to play the draglines and pitch nickels onto saucers to get the big stuffed toys that never came, never came, or to pay the small start money at the hootchy-kootchy tent where the woman danced for half a dollar on a wooden platform outside and a dollar inside, except that the boys were said to be too young to be inside, the boys who would hunt. Luckily there were holes in the canvas that could be enlarged only a little with a pocketknife, and the inside was lighted with a large bulb hanging in the middle that made it easy to see all the parts of the dance until Sonny Burton pushed too hard and the bouncer inside saw the canvas bulge and came out to chase us away.

Summer died hard, setting pins at the bowling alley where the pits were so hot Kyle Nova passed out, and a man who had too much beer threw the ball anyway and the boys thought it killed Kyle. The man had to leave when all the pinsetters came out of the pits and started throwing pins at him even though Kyle wasn't killed but only had a broken finger. The boys set his alley for him for three weeks until he could work again while he sat up in the open back window above the pits and talked about going all the way with Clair Severson who had big ones, which the boys found later was a lie but it didn't matter because it was a good story anyway

and got better when Clair found out about it and hit Kyle with a bicycle, a whole bicycle, and like to killed him.

Summer died hard when people sat on their porches of an evening under yellow light and listened to the moths hitting the bulb and drank basement beer out of quart jars and talked of working at the grain elevator or hatchery until the young ones were asleep in the porch swing and had to be carried in and put to bed without awakening.

Summer died hard.

But it happened in one night. Somebody would reach for a tomato or flip a cigarette out the back window of the bowling alley between balls and it would be there.

The cool. The fall cool. A corner of a touch of cool air, a chill on the back of the hand, a puff of breath that showed, a kiss on the temple from the north, from all the way north where it is always cool.

Fall had come.

And there is nothing else then—nothing else but hunting grouse.

But first the excitement, and the excitement begins with equipment.

The boys who hunted, the orphans of the woods, did not have money, and so many of the ways to hunt now were not available to them. Auto-loading shotguns, super-trained dogs, cars, special coats, vests to hold shells or birds, boots—all of that was not available then.

Choices had to be made. A new pair of boots cost close to six dollars, half a week's wages setting pins and selling papers to the drunks in the bars along the river. A box of .22 long-rifle cartridges was thirty cents. A pair of boots was the same as twenty boxes of long rifles. Twenty boxes at fifty shells a box was a thousand rounds, and a boy without money could hunt an entire fall and winter on a thousand rounds; shoot cans and grouse and rabbits and hunt until spring and use any other money for school clothes or food or a book, sometimes a book. On hunting or fishing or the woods.

We had to use what equipment we could get. Most had a cheap single-shot .22 rifle. New they could be bought for eleven dollars and ninety-five cents, but it was always possible to find a used one in somebody's garage or hanging on a nail on a back porch for two or three dollars. Work guns. Kill-the-steer-for-slaughter guns. Guns for shooting the skunk in the henhouse, the weasel in the coop, the stray cat with the duckling, the rats killing baby rabbits—utility guns for everything from rabid dogs to a needed deer. They were not necessarily good rifles. A rough maple or even pine stock and a stamped metal trigger; hard to load, with a knob that had to be pulled back to cock the rifle when it was time to fire, and a safety so crude that it practically ensured accidental discharge. First gun—no, second gun. First was a Daisy Red Ryder lever-action BB gun with the leather thong on the side, but the first real gun, the first rifle, was the .22 single-shot. And the feeling that came with the rifle; the knowing that came with it, the way of it to go back and forward in time. To go back until it was the same rifle as the Minutemen held at Concord, the same as the flintlocks used to hunt when hunting was all, and to go forward from the .22 and the boy until he was a man standing in a rank in the hot Colorado sun with other men who were once boys while a sergeant slammed an M1 .30 caliber air-cooled semiautomatic shoulder weapon into his hands and told him how it would be to kill another man with such a weapon—the same rifle. The same boy. The same man.

For the boys it was also usually the only gun. Everything else was too expensive. Some boys had even older rifles, antique rolling-block Stevens .22 rifles with an external hammer. They were loaded by dropping a small block and (usually) picking the fired cartridge case out the rear with a pocketknife; rifles that spit back every time they were fired, and left pits of powder in the eye that lasted until the boys were men, and then old men, who would be bankers or write books.

One boy had a J. C. Higgins model .410 single-shot break-open shotgun that his father had won in a raffle. He was the envy of all with the new gun but the shells were fantastically expensive—a dollar eighty a box for only twenty-five shells—and when he shot something it was full of BB shot that had to be spit out when you ate the meat. Still, the gun was a thing of beauty and easy to load and shoot, and even the boys who sneered at it and talked of spitting BBs and how it didn't take skill to shoot things with it, even those who knew it all and could speak with the corner of the mouth lifted, secretly wanted such a gun, such a new gun to hunt with.

One boy had a Mossberg .22 semiautomatic rifle that would take sixteen rounds in a tube in the stock and had a covered front sight and a molded strip in the handgrip with places for the fingers. It was an elegant rifle—everybody agreed—and had been designed during the Second World War to teach shooting to soldiers, which gave it extra mystique. But it weighed a great deal and everybody thought it made the owner a bad shot because if he missed with the first there was the second and if he missed with the second there was the third and on and on until he had spit out sixteen shells and missed with them all. With the single-shot there was a tendency to wait just that half a second to ensure a clear hit, and generally the waiting made the owner a better shot. That was, at least, the expressed feeling among the boys who could not own the better rifle and had to stick with the single-shots because of bad luck or lack of money.

Whatever the gun, the first cool night in September, when there would be frost on the edges of leaves in the morning, the night before the first hunting morning, the world changed.

It was not slow, this change—and in some ways it was inside the boys. Summer died that night and the knowledge that there would be grouse hunting the next morning changed everything, changed the whole world.

Suddenly everything that had lain dormant all summer, every little thing about fall and hunting, became important.

During the day in school fall stories from the year before are taken up where they were left off the previous autumn. This grouse that was taken, that grouse that got away, six, eight shots and all misses, one impossible shot and the grouse fell. Notes are passed talking about the forty-acre stand of poplar and pine four miles south of town and how it must be full of grouse because it has been left alone all summer, how there must be fifteen, twenty, fifty, a hundred grouse in there, hiding in there, just waiting to be taken. Notes passed and taken on the state of equipment. This rifle is that good, this sight is knocked loose and needs to be checked—endless talks, notes about shells, triggers, guns, bullets.

And the day crawls, doesn't crawl, stops right in

the middle of study hall. The large white clock on the wall with the big numbers and the second hand that normally moves—slowly, but moves—stops dead.

Somebody has to drop a notebook on the floor or cough or fart to relieve the tension and get the clock moving again. The clock drags itself around, staggering toward the end of the day and still it isn't over, still it doesn't hurry.

At home, hidden from prying eyes, is the equipment for hunting. It is there, waiting, but there is another variable to handle first—parents. Parents who may have other plans for the next day like school or chores; or worse, parents who drink and say no to all things, no matter what is asked.

It is better to hide from them and wait while the day grinds along until they are so drunk it is safe to go home, to go inside and prepare for the next day.

Sleep is impossible.

The gun is checked, rechecked, the boots oiled with Crisco, bullets wiped and tied into the sock that holds them, then it is untied and they are rechecked again, three, four more times, and the clock next to the bunk, the old brass clock with the hammer that gongs back and forth between two bells, is still sitting on nine o'clock. Like the school clock it doesn't move. The alarm is muted with bits of cloth so it won't awaken the parents and no sooner are the eyes closed than they open in worry:

Will the alarm be heard when it goes off? *If* it goes off? What if it goes off at the wrong time and it is too late to meet the boys down by the hatchery and they go alone and the first day of hunting is ruined because it will be necessary to hunt alone and it is hard to hunt alone?

What if that?

What if?

Sleep comes. At last it comes, but it is not deep, and it is not dreamless sleep. The mind works all the time sleep is tried, and it keeps waiting for the bell on the alarm. Waiting so hard that in ten minutes it awakens, forces eyes to open, forces muscles to contract, forces the body to sit up, look at the alarm.

Ten minutes have passed. That's all.

Sleep comes again.

Ten more minutes.

And so the night goes—bouncing from ten-minute sleep to ten-minute sleep until at last deep sleep comes, deep drooling-out-the-corner-of-the-mouth sleep; so deep that it is not possible to hear the alarm when it goes off and were it not for one of the boys stopping by and tapping on the window, opening day would be lost. But Jimmy comes by on his way and throws small rocks at the window and wakens the sleeper, ends the deep sleep.

Then up.

Pitch dark. Black. So dark and black that it seems incredible that day could ever come. Quietly down the hallway past the parents' door lest they awaken, to open the back door and let Jimmy in. Quieter still, a frying pan on the stove, not scraping or clanging because, God, if they awaken they'll ruin it all, ruin everything for the rest of life if they come out because of kitchen noise. Jimmy sitting in the corner, leaning his head against the wall with an impatient look on his face because *he* was on time, *he* was able to get up early, *he* had his gear and food all ready, and it was important, it was everything, to get out of town and into the woods while it was still dark, to not waste a moment of daylight non-hunting. A little lard in the pan and four eggs from the icebox, no, five eggs to fry until they are burned on the outside edges, burned and crisp and crackling with the yolks and parts of the whites still runny. Pepper dusted over them, and salt, three eggs eaten out of the pan with pieces of bread to soak up the grease and yolk while Jimmy sits in the corner glaring, angry; no talk, not even whispers, just sitting there, fuming. Two more eggs folded into bread and wrapped in wax paper and tucked into a paper sack and rolled into a jacket pocket for later.

Then gear, boots on, jacket, hat, shells—make certain of shells, check the shells twice, three times —rifle, gloves.

And out.

It is still dark, almost pitch—Jimmy needn't have brewed up—and there is new frost, first frost lining the edges of trees and grass, the tops of propane tanks.

Air catches on the sides of the nostrils, cold, crisp, no smells—clean air—and for a moment the boys stop and listen to the town, pull the air in and listen, looking at the dark sky and the glow from the town lights.

Then away.

Down Fifth Street four blocks to the railroad, walking easily, rifles over shoulders not loaded, not loaded until the woods.

Across the tracks, then turn and move with them, talking in low sounds, breath "whuffing" out in front of faces, sting of cold on cheeks, the sandwiches still warm in the jacket pocket, warm against the side, and Jimmy speaking of a hunt before, last year, year before, talking about working along the river and catching mallards, something about ducks but not all clear . . . fuzzy words in the dark morning.

Past the coal tower where they used to store coal to fill the steam-fired locomotives, looming up like a monster in the dark, a roosting place for pigeons to be hunted later, not with guns but with slingshots using marbles, hunted in the dark and coal dust, to come home flat black except for eyes and loaded with pigeons for pies and roasting.

Then to the hatchery, where three other boys are waiting, Harvey's face glowing as he smokes an Old

Gold corktip—he is the only one to smoke steady yet, though all will try it because all agree it makes Harvey look older—and the boys set off walking in single file.

Off the tracks, walking faster now because there is grayness in the east—not light yet, just not as dark, but dawn will come fast when it comes, and light in town is wasted; light anywhere but in the woods is wasted.

Three blocks to the Fourth Street bridge, over the river with ice along the edges where the water is still. A muskrat slides off a log into the water with a soft splash. Across and then left, past a cornfield, another, then along half a mile of dirt road. Well out of town now, but still another half a mile to the woods. The first stand of woods. Walking silently now. To talk is to scare the game. One foot flat in front of the other, just walking, moving through the early morning.

Still not light but definitely gray now and the edges of things starting to show; bushes, trees, the side of the road. Frost-rimmed and colder now, just before dawn, the coldest time of the day; breath comes in spurts, and Jimmy whispers there is a hunting moon, which seems dumb because there is no moon at all but maybe that's what he means.

Finally to the woods, the first hunting woods.

It is a stand of hazel brush and poplar, fifth, sixth growth—maybe tenth. Nobody knows. It has been logged for paper and trash wood so many times it is little more than a thick bramble covering forty or so acres. There are swamps and some balsam here and there and deer and rabbits and, of course, grouse.

The boys stop there, wait for a moment: Wayne, who is often quiet and shoots well but doesn't brag; Sonny, who shoots well but does brag and lies, so nobody listens to him; and Harvey, who as far as anybody can remember has never hit a single animal that he has aimed at in his entire life though he has a good semiautomatic rifle and seems to spray bullets every time he sees a grouse or rabbit; and Bennie and Sam. We wear hand-me-downs. Old coats, old boots—none can afford good, new equipment— shells carried in pockets, army surplus ammo belts. Two boys wear sheepskin flight helmets though the day will probably be warm and they will swelter in them. Runny noses, half of us sniffling, hawking, spitting. Nods, greetings, hushed teases: ". . . I see Jimmy got your ass up" and ". . . spend all night pulling your pud?"

More plans are made. Plans *must* be made. Not original hunting plans. They were done in school, at the bowling alley in the pits, walking home from school, hiding from drunken parents in basements.

But immediate plans. Field plans.

How to hunt the woods.

It is always the same. Every year. Two boys with good weapons on either end to catch the animals that try to go around the sweep-through. The same two boys. Harvey with the semiautomatic who has never hit anything on one end, and Bennie with the single-shot four-ten on the other end because he dreams of getting a good wing shot on a flying grouse, and everybody has at least once had to duck because Bennie tracked on a grouse and let go without thinking where he was aiming. Two boys have pits from the shot that went through coats and sweaters and made it into skin. With him working the right end of the sweep, only those on his left will have to worry when a bird gets up. Sam claims to hold the record at dropping—hitting the ground flat in the split second between the time Bennie cocks the four-ten and actually pulls the trigger—but others swear to have actually ducked the shot, dropped between the moment when he fires and the one when the shot arrives. It doesn't matter who is on the end really, because no animals ever try to get around them. It is a myth, but still it is part of the hunting plan in the early morning just before the hunt starts and must every year be discussed.

This boy on the left, this one next, this one next, everybody moving as quietly as possible, no yelling or other loud noises, lined up on the dirt road along the edge of the woods, bolts pulled back, .22 long rifle loaded, bolts in, safety on, barrel up, ready.

And it is still too dark to hunt.

So it is, standing, waiting to move, too far from

the next boy to talk, watching the sun slide with agonizing slowness up over the woods to show first individual trees, then limbs, and, finally, leaves and small branches; to stand and wait, half asleep, numb with sleep, waiting for the light. To wait, to stand and wait, and try to make things happen, and they will not happen.

To hunt grouse.

First Shot

There are worlds to live in, all different, all important, all complete. At night there is the world at the bowling alley, back in the dark pits soaked in sweat, deafened by the crashing of balls slamming into hardwood pins, a cigarette hanging always out the side of the mouth, naked from the waist up, working two alleys screaming joyful curses at the other pinsetters while earning the unheard-of wealth of seven cents a line, eleven cents if it's league night; setting two alleys each night without a break until eleven-thirty, every weeknight, earning twelve dollars a week. With tips that they throw down the gutters if they get a good game, sometimes a dollar in the fingerhole of the ball if they are trying to impress a girl wearing tight slacks—and inspiring almost terminal lust in the pinsetters when she throws her ball, leaning over without thinking of the view she is presenting the four pairs of testosterone-driven eyes in the dark of the pits. Or perhaps she knows, like Willy said, knows and really wants the boys in the pit to see while they slam back and forth from alley to alley, scooping up the ball to flip it carelessly into the ball-return chute and bending to grab two and sometimes three pins in each hand to slide them easily into the pin racks before jerking them down in one motion, all in one motion.

There is the world of the bars. Before setting pins and sometimes on the weekends later at night, working through the bars to sell newspapers; waiting until the men in the bar get juiced to sell more papers, to hustle more money; the bars where the men drink beer out of the bottles with water running down the side in droplets, standing at the bar with no stools while they talk of work and women and woods and fishing and women and cars and trucks and women in raw terms, naked words.

There is the world of home. Where they fight and drink and scream and make up and fight and drink and scream; the world where it is necessary to hide in the basement of the tenement building in back of the furnace, around in back on the old easy chair with the springs sticking through the stuffing and a single light hanging with the filaments showing and read, read books to take away thoughts; fly them away to other worlds, other times, other lives that are better than the life in the basement.

There is the world of the back alleys. Where in

some mysterious way it is always dark, and pennies are pitched and sometimes on dares or challenges more than pennies—nickels, a dime, but never larger because a quarter or half dollar is simply too much money to waste, to gamble; to work all night setting pins for seven cents a line and then bet the farm, shoot the wad, dump the load all on a pitched coin in an alley is too much. Alleys where much is decided by scuffling, called fighting then but always ending before anybody had more than a blackened eye or bloody nose; before weapons, except for Tip, who had a switchblade his father brought back from Germany where it was said he took it off a dead German during the War except that on the blade it said MADE IN U.S.A., which everybody ignored because we wanted to believe it came off a dead German killed by Tip's father, who was a for-real war hero. It made a better story. Tip never used the switchblade except to show off because he pulled it on Wayne Hallock once and Wayne hit him so hard with a garbage-can lid that Tip swore he saw God in the stars—that's how he put it, "I saw God-in-the-stars." The alley world where it was always dark and dreams were always low and pride always high.

But the world of the woods, the world when the road is left, stepped from softly, the world in the trees in the early morning with low fog hanging and ice crystals glimmering on tree limbs—the world of the first morning of the first day of the first hunt is a world so old, so wonderfully ancient that it is always completely new.

Everything changes.

The light is not the same light that comes from the sun. It starts in fusion, is born in cosmic explosions and heat, but when it at last reaches the woods it is altered, shaped, bent and warped and molded into something close to sculpture. The morning light wraps a tree, catches the ice, becomes a dance, almost light-music. Things seen every day—a limb, a leaf, stones, swamp grass—all take on a change with the morning light and it stops not just one boy but all the boys; stops all of us just inside the woods.

Stops us to change.

No longer the town boys, no longer the drunk-parent boys or the alley boys or the bar boys or the bowling alley boys—not any of those now, not even boys now. Oh no.

Deerslayer.

Last of the Mohicans.

Buffalo Bill.

The light changes the woods and the woods change us. We aren't wearing hand-me-downs or army surplus ammo belts, not carrying two-dollar worn-out .22 single-shots with cracked stocks, not standing in worn boots with too-large canvas hunting caps stuffed with newspaper to keep them above the ears.

We are *hunters*.

Buckskin-clad, eyes alert, rifle (it could easily be a Kentucky, a flintlock with curly maple stock and silver dressing) poised, balanced gracefully up and out to the left, the oiled barrel catching the same morning light while we crouch/step/flow into the woods; part of it, part of the light, the cold, the leaves on the ground, the air, part of it all.

Hunters.

And there are things to hunt.

There are the grouse.

Some say grouse are little more than a really dumb wild chicken, but they are wrong. Grouse live in the woods alone, without clothes, without fire, with nothing to help them but themselves, and they have not only survived, they have thrived, grown.

Everything that eats meat hunts them. Fox, wolf, lynx, bobcat, raccoon (sometimes), wild house cats, neighborhood dogs, snakes (when they are chicks), skunks, weasels, owls, hawks, and boys with .22 rifles on the first morning of hunting.

They are at the same time easy to hunt and almost impossible to hunt. Later there are rules, later in life there are ethics to this business, and no hunter worth his salt would ever shoot one sitting, would always try for a wing shot and very often miss, if he hunted them at all.

But not the boys.

With a .22 rifle it is impossible to shoot them

flying, and so they must be hunted sitting, and over the eons, over the hundreds of thousands of years they have existed, grouse have learned one thing to absolute perfection.

They have learned to sit.

It is an art, the way they sit. With their coloration—speckled gray to brown, bars and stripes mixed with spots—they blend perfectly with where they choose to hide: in brush, at the base of clumps of willows amidst fallen leaves and grass. They sit still—no, more than still. They become what they are in; become a part of the earth, cease to exist as a bird, as something alive.

It is entirely possible to look right at a grouse, know that it is there, have it pointed out and still not see it—and continue to not see it until it explodes into flight beneath your feet in the thunder that comes from air compressing between their wings and bodies when they fly.

Tip says often, every fall he says it, says it again and again until everybody is sick of it but it is still true; he says that hunting grouse—except he calls them partridge, which they're not, because articles in *Field and Stream* said they're not—is like hunting morel mushrooms in the spring. For morels everything must be perfect; a wet spring followed by soft, warm weather, all well before the grass comes green or any plants have yet recovered from winter enough so they can grow and hide the mushrooms, and then on one night, a soft spring warm night, they come.

Except it is hard to see them. Overnight they come, little Christmas-tree-shaped, spear-point, gnome-hat mushrooms pop up on the north sides of shallow slopes and along the south banks of lakes and rivers in the brush and willows, but for some reason they are almost invisible. They can be thick all around and not show themselves until something happens, some mysterious magical thing triggers, and the shape enters the brain, the little triangle shape, and then it is impossible to *not* see them and morels are everywhere, bags of them, to fry in fresh butter and eat with fresh bread.

Just so with grouse.

It isn't that the grouse are seen, are hunted, are known, as much as the place where the grouse *sits* is seen, known. Less a shape than a bend in the light, a corner, a shadow that makes the brain think of grouse.

And it is there.

Right *there*.

Sitting still, they freeze and don't move, don't breathe, don't blink, and the old-timers are full of stories of how they don't move. Sit on a limb until you reach up and grab them, fool birds, sit on a nest while you reach under and take eggs, sit on a branch while the branch is sawed off and taken out of the woods and home and nailed to a barn wall and the neighbors are called to come and see the stupid bird sitting on the limb on the barn wall.

They have lived by sitting, and it is what allows boys with old single-shot .22s to hunt them, take them, eat them.

But not always.

There is something about their stillness, their solidity that causes a frantic feeling, a need to hurry, to make the shot before they can fly and so the rifle is raised and the barrel aimed in the general direction of the grouse and the trigger jerked.

To miss.

"What's that?" Somebody yells from down the line. "What the hell are you shooting at?"

"Grouse."

"Did you get him?"

A cry that, a tease, a curse.

"Did you get him?"

"Did you get him?"

A vicious question, a question of worth, a challenge question.

"Did you get him?"

"No."

"What the hell. . . ."

And the grouse holds while fumbling fingers jerk the bolt of the rifle open. The empty shell does not extract. Close the bolt and jerk it open again and the shell still does not come out.

And the grouse holds. There, ten, eight, four feet

away at the base of a willow standing perfectly solid the grouse still holds.

Out with the pocketknife. Swearing under the breath. Damn gun never works. The same swear as all hunters when they miss. It is the gun, the bow, the spear, the club that is deficient.

Pick at the jammed empty shell casing with the pocketknife. Pick. Pick.

The grouse holds.

Finally the empty case slides out. Drop the knife. It can be found later. A new shell from a jacket pocket. Jammed in. No, wrong end. Backwards. There, lead in the bore, pushed in with a thumb.

Still the grouse holds.

Raise the rifle, aim quickly, pull the trigger.

Nothing. Forgot to pull back the cocking spring. Reach up, jerk it back and let go before the trigger engages.

The rifle fires.

Well away from the grouse, a foot above, two feet above.

"Did you get him?"

"Did you *get* him?"

Damn—a hiss under the breath, a curse at the soul of the rifle, the man who invented the rifle, the men who invent all rifles, the souls of all grouse.

Still the grouse holds.

Another jam. Kneel slowly to pick up the pocketknife where it was dropped, and now at last it is too much.

While kneeling, one hand groping for the knife, off-balance, the eyes are dropped for one second, less, a part of a second, and that is when it happens.

The grouse detonates, blows from the ground in the sound of thunder, and it startles so completely that it is hard not to pee, not to scream and pee and run, and then it is done.

"Did you *get* him?"

A hesitation, a breath, a lifetime excuse.

"No. I missed him. He flew."

Many grouse will come and many will be missed and some will be taken. They will be eaten stuffed with dandelion greens and baked with new red potatoes fresh from the garden garnished with fresh goat butter and salt. They will be eaten cold from a plate with fingers while winter comes and eaten baked with strips of bacon over them to keep the meat moist and eaten stuffed with wild rice taken over the side of a canoe in the late summer and eaten with corn on the cob dripping with butter and salt. They will be eaten for almost all the falls that come, and each and every time a bite is taken, each time the taste comes from the rich breast meat, the memory will be there.

"Did you *get* him?"

"No. I missed him. He flew."

Bow Hunting

All of hunting was everything when fall came; there didn't seem to be anything else. School, setting pins, even girls—all of it faded compared to hunting.

But bow hunting was more demanding than other forms, took more effort, more art, and so became perhaps more important.

This was in the time before compound bows or aluminum or fiberglass arrows or even full recurve bows. Laminated glass bows were just coming into use and so were very expensive for the boys— twenty-nine ninety-five for a semi-recurve Bear Cub (the cheapest Bear bow available), which amounted to three weeks setting pins and not spending anything on candy, food, clothes, or movies at the Carousel Theater where movie and a popcorn and candy bar could go close to fifty cents.

In other words, buying a bow was an impossibility.

For that reason most of the boys did not have modern equipment. Straight wooden bows were carried by most and could be purchased through catalogs for seven or eight dollars. They usually seemed to come at about thirty-five-pounds' pull but lost it fast, because once they were strung and carried strung for a day of hunting the wood would take a "set" and lose some of its spring tension. A more accurate pound weight would probably be in the neighborhood of twenty-eight pounds unless one of the slightly more expensive fiber-backed bows could be found. These were a stage before laminate fiberglass bows and, while not as good as equipment now, were some better than plain wood.

Most boys couldn't afford to buy any bow and made their own for shop projects where the best wood—lemonwood—could be bought for as little as a dollar through the school. Mr. Halverson, who taught shop, also hunted with a bow and would help shave and balance the limbs to get proper pull and true flight, and it is hard to think of bows without seeing Mr. Halverson's hand pulling the small shaving plane along a bow-limb and the curls of wood coming up over his scarred thumb while he smiled and sucked on an unlit pipe and talked of moose hunting in Canada or trying to wing-shoot pheasants with arrows in South Dakota.

Arrows were a problem as well. They cost so much to buy "factory-made"—twenty-eight cents apiece—that buying was simply out of the question. Six, seven, even ten arrows could be lost in a day while hunting, and to lose that much wealth in one day was inconceivable.

A hundred cedar shafts could be purchased mail-order for two dollars and fourteen cents. Nocks to take the string were half a cent each, and for points it was found that empty .38 special-cartridge cases slid perfectly and glued on the wooden shafts and made as good a blunt—the best point for hunting small game—as could be purchased from archery suppliers. The police department had boxes of empty .38 special cases from target firing and would always part with twenty or so when asked.

Mail-order feathers were expensive, but they were always slaughtering turkeys down at the hatchery by the railroad tracks, and they would let boys stand as the turkeys were hooked up to the overhead track and pull wing feathers off as the turkeys were sent into the killing room. One afternoon would give enough feathers for a whole year.

The feathers could be held between two thin boards and the spine sanded off to make a base to glue to the arrow in just a few moments. Ben Pearson Archery sold a clamp-jig to put feathers on three at a time for two dollars, and it was guaranteed to last a lifetime no matter how many arrows were made. Duco cement was used to glue the feathers on, and they could be cut into a streamlined shape with sewing scissors as long as a mother didn't know it.

The arrows wobbled a bit and sometimes broke easily, and often—almost always—missed, but they only cost four cents each, and if by a miracle they were brought onto the target right they got the job done.

The sleeve out of an old leather flight jacket left over from the war made a good quiver, held on with an old belt over the shoulder, and as many as twenty arrows could be carried into the woods for hunting.

Hunting was different with a bow.

With a gun anything was possible, ranges could vary, targets as well. Once the initial excitement was over and aiming could be accomplished, the little .22 single-shot became deadly anywhere from point blank to pushing fifty yards—using long-rifle cartridges—and it would take anything from grouse and rabbits to a deer or bear (those larger animals cannot be legally taken with a .22, but have been killed that way, as well as moose and elk). For many years the .22 was known as a camp gun or work gun and was all many woods-runners—trappers, guides, lumber-scalers—would carry, using it to get camp meat as well as for protection. But the gun removes the animal from consideration in a way, makes the activity less hunting and more killing, and makes it possible to hunt an animal without knowing as much about it as bow hunting requires.

Hunting with a bow changes all things, even the way to move. With the bows then used, and the crude arrows, twenty yards was a long shot, an almost unheard-of shot on grouse or rabbits. Fifteen, twenty *feet* was more realistic—and closer was better.

To get that close to game it is mandatory to know the game, to study it, to know that rabbits come to the edges of clearings in the early morning or late afternoon or that grouse will move toward gravel (for their gizzards) in the evenings before they roost so they can digest their food while they sleep. Hunting with a bow it must be known that having a dog will make grouse jump up sooner but they will land in trees to avoid the dog and might give a good tree-shot; or that a dog will run a rabbit but rabbits are territorial and hate to leave their usual area so will run in a circle, and if you stand and wait they sometimes will come back around and might give you a chance for a running shot—difficult to hit but challenging to try. . . .

The real beauty of hunting with a bow is that there is no noise. A shot doesn't scare all the game in the area, and even the animal being shot at often isn't startled. Because it is so hard to hit anything, especially something as small as a grouse—smaller yet when it is remembered that it must be hit in the

middle of the middle or the arrow will brush through the feathers without hitting the body of the grouse—it is easy to shoot all the arrows carried without hitting the bird. Failure is much more common than success. The area that must be caught by the arrow is only as big as a fist, and if the bird is twenty feet away, sitting in willows or brush, hitting something that small with a wooden bow and wooden homemade arrows, driving the back end of a .38 special blunt into a target that small is close to impossible. Once I shot fourteen arrows at a grouse sitting at the base of a clump of willows not ten feet away, every arrow I had with me, and the grouse was still there, and stayed there while I carefully reached forward, pulled one of the arrows out of the ground, nocked it on the string and shot one more time—this time brushing the grouse enough to startle it and make it fly away.

But when it is learned, when the bow is understood and used as it was meant to be used, used as an extension of the mind and within its limits, the bow can be deadly. When shooting a true bow— not a sight-mounted compound with aluminum arrows (really almost a different kind of gun)—a true bow with no sight, it takes more practice, practice, until the fingers are calloused from the string and the shoulders are corded with the effort, driving the shafts into hay bales again and again. When it is done enough, when the practice has gone on so long that everything is automatic, a strange thing happens.

The arrow becomes alive. Without a sight, when it is at full draw and tucked back under the chin, the wood of the arrow sings and it is alive and the flight can be "felt." Looking down the shaft the center of the center, *inside* the core of the center of the middle of the target can be seen. When that feeling is right, when the arrow is part of the mind and the mind is part of the arrow and the release comes smoothly and the string takes the arrow correctly, the arrow has no choice but to go to that place, the center of the aimed place.

Some hunts with bows were disasters. No rabbits or grouse, all the arrows either lost because they snaked beneath the grass and couldn't be found or broke when they hit stumps, to leave the boys walking home with empty quivers and no meat. Sometimes all the boys would hunt for all the day, and there would be one rabbit, one grouse.

But not always. There was a time when all the wolves and coyotes and fox had been trapped out by the state—trying to control without knowing how to control. Since the wolves, coyotes, and fox were the only thing really holding the rabbits down, and since rabbits reproduce like, well, rabbits, the numbers became staggering. It was common to walk down a mile of dirt country road in the fall and count fifty, a hundred rabbits just sitting in the ditch or jumping back into the woods. They began to get tularemia—a disease transmittable to humans —and the state decided it was necessary to hunt the rabbits out, or at least take them down to a manage-able number. Since almost no adults hunted them, the job fell on the boys, and it came at about the time bow hunting was at its peak. The rabbits were not wasted; after being checked for the disease and found clear, the carcasses were used for orphanages and poor farms. This was long before welfare or food stamps, and all extra or confiscated game was used for orphans and the poor.

Nobody counted all the rabbits taken, but limits were not checked, nor encouraged, and many, many thousands of them were killed.

On a day the boys were using wood bows and homemade arrows, in the high time of that hunt with empty .38 special-cartridge cases for blunts— on one single day the boys worked an eighty-acre stand of brush and poplar and took over a hundred rabbits. A hundred rabbits to get and tie the back legs to each other to drape across bicycles and cart back to Eckert Feed and Fur Supply, where old man Eckert paid a dime a rabbit.

Later there were larger hunts. Later there were days using .22 rifles when three and four hundred rabbits were taken—all carried into town draped over hand-pushed bicycles to be sold for a dime each. The state paid the money through old man

Eckert and then gave the meat to the poor and orphans, and it was not until years later that the boys found out Eckert was getting a quarter a rabbit and pocketing fifteen cents a rabbit for himself. And it was not for many years that the boys found out Eckert was rich and owned vast holdings of land west of town, many hundreds of acres, the same acres the boys hunted; not for many years that the boys found out that old man Eckert had lived through the death camps in Europe and now spent almost all of the money he made giving the boys a dime a rabbit and keeping fifteen cents a rabbit— spent all of the money he made helping other survivors of the camps find a life.

But none of the later hunts with the rifle or even still later hunts for love or hunts for life or hunts in the army or hunts in art equaled the hunt with bows when the rabbits were so many that they filled the woods and ditches and roads.

The first deer hunt with a bow started almost a year before the actual hunt took place.

A deer is so big a thing to kill with an arrow, so big and beautiful a thing, that the preparation becomes perhaps more important than the hunt itself, a kind of prayer.

Sometimes the rabbits died fast when the blunt took them, and always the grouse died fast, but there were times when the rabbits were hit wrong and then the death came not so fast, not so clean, more like a natural death than a hunting death, more like a wolf death or coyote death or fox death or weasel death or owl death for the rabbit—a death to make the hunter think of the animal. And when that happened, when the arrow hitting the rabbit did not end him fast but let him scream in the high-pitched death scream that rabbits have, it made deer hunting seem impossible.

There was too much animal for an arrow. It was forgotten then that almost all animals had given lives to arrows; that men in armor, men in blue cavalry, men in leather leggings had all died from arrows, died in hundreds, died in thousands, fell in rows to wooden shafts and steel or stone points.

A deer seemed so big. But then the excitement set in, a boy told another boy that somebody last year had taken an enormous buck—a six-, eight-, ten-pointer that dressed out at a hundred eighty, hundred ninety, two twenty-five pounds; that the buck had been taken with one arrow shot at forty, fifty, eighty yards and the deer just dropped.

Just dropped.

Clean.

That's how the boy said it—like some are dirtier than others; like there is a clean way to kill, to die. As if such a thing could be.

Soon it is too much, the excitement, and there comes a decision to hunt deer with a bow.

Preparation takes time—a year—and money. Practice is vital. The only way to bring a deer down is to get a good shot, a proper shot, a correct shot.

There are many bad shots. An arrow through the stomach, an arrow through a leg, an arrow through a rump, an arrow across the front of the chest, an arrow across the edge of the neck—all of these could kill the deer, let the deer bleed to death, but not kill it right away. A gut shot will kill but it might take hours, days, and if there is no blood trail to follow, the deer will wander off and die where it cannot be found. It will not be a clean kill.

There are many more bad places to hit a deer than there are proper places and so, practice. Cardboard cutouts of deer life-size are made and pinned to hay bales and shot at until they hang in tatters. Again and again at ten, twenty, even thirty yards the cardboard is hit, hit properly in its cardboard heart, hit correctly in its cardboard lungs—hit again and again until the cardboard deer dies a clean cardboard death.

But it is not the same when life is real—not ever the same.

First there is the matter of the arrow.

A deer cannot be killed with a blunt that works on a rabbit or a grouse. It takes a special point—a broadhead.

But broadheads are expensive—a quarter each just for the points—and they bend and get their edges ruined easily, so it is not feasible to practice with them. On top of that, the broadheads used then were just simple, flat two-bladed points that were difficult to mount on the shaft straight. Because they were flat-sided and quite large they tended to "fight the feathers," and cause the arrow to plane off in strange directions. Tip swore he shot one once that went all the way around in a circle and almost killed him but nobody saw it and almost nobody believed him.

Because the broadheads cost so much and break so easily and are seldom shot at targets, there are terrible problems with accuracy that make it extremely difficult to get a deer, but still the attempt continues.

Still the preparation goes on.

Each broadhead is mounted as straight as possible, glued with melted ferrule cement that dries hard as iron, and is then sharpened, and sharpened, and sharpened. . . .

For a broadhead to work it must cut effortlessly.

Even primitive man knew this. The boys once found a stone arrowhead in a block of dried and cracked clay near the edge of a river. The head was of black flint and shined like new when wet. Wayne held it up to the light and said, "Look, the light comes through," and as he twisted it to see the sun better, the old edges, buried in clay for hundreds, maybe thousands of years, the scalloped and shaped edges, slid in his grasp and nearly took a finger off with one small slicing action.

There were none of the razor-blade inserts when we hunted that make the modern heads so deadly, and the flatheads used then had to be hand-sharpened.

First a small file was used to shape a shallow, gradual edge on each side of the point. Considering that there may be twelve points—if such extravagance can be afforded—and each point has four edge-sides to file, the initial honing down can take considerable time. A week, two weeks can be spent, every spare moment used to file the heads. After the filing there is the actual sharpening, using an oilstone, and since no head is good unless it is as sharp as a razor and can literally shave the hair off an arm, this process may take longer than the filing. (It is, really, never done; Tip and Wayne argue that the points will get dull—lose their fine edge—just being exposed to air and they carry small stones while they're hunting and resharpen the heads during breaks or sometimes while walking down a road or —once with Wayne—while sitting in church, much to the distress of Wayne's mother, who hit him so hard with a hymnal he thought she'd dropped a pew on him.)

Much was not understood then about hunting deer with a bow. It is known now about camouflage, about hiding and hunting from stands. But then most people just walked quietly through the woods until a shot presented itself. Those who could afford them bought soft leather moccasins to make the walking silent—or as silent as it could be on dry leaves and grass—but most made their own moccasins from patterns found in magazines and books.

But even then the need for silence was understood, and the boys practiced walking constantly, feet straight ahead, weight down on the ball of the foot to step slowly, carefully, silently ahead, stopping every three or four steps to look into, into the *inside* of the woods, to look for a line, a curve, or a slight motion that could mean a deer.

It often never comes.

Days can be spent walking through woods, the bow held in the left hand with a broadhead nocked to the string, one finger holding the arrow against the bow, walking and looking and smelling and listening—waiting.

Waiting.

And sometimes if movement is not right or the boys aren't lucky—sometimes a whole season can be spent looking, waiting, hunting for nothing; nothing except walking through the beauty of autumn days in the thick forest, moving through color and clean air and the soft light of a million dappled leaves while the act of hunting forces all the things seen, all the beauty into the mind, but it is not until later, until years and a life later, that it is understood. When it becomes known that the reason for hunting is not the deer, never has been the deer, never would be the deer; the reason for hunting is just that: to hunt.

To hunt the sun, the wind, the trees—to hunt the beauty. In time, in memory, it all becomes more important than the deer, than the quarry.

Than the kill.

When it comes, it is not so much, and still it is more than anything before it and makes a sadness that will not go away even with life, even with all of life.

Everything, every aspect of it is remembered for all the rest of the time there is; everything.

It is early morning.

It is early morning and there are no clouds so the sun comes cleanly up in the east and filters new light through the chill air to make everything seem overly defined, almost to having cutting edges. Leaves are not just part of trees, part of the forest, but jump out in the morning air like small paintings, each a work of art alone. A rock catches light and becomes alive, seems to move; a tree limb stands out against the sky like an etching, caught and held in the new sun.

It is early morning and cold enough so the air sticks in the nose and sounds seem more clear, sharper than they do at other times; a grouse moves, leaves rustle, and it could be anything—a moose, a bear, a deer.

There is a deer, but not yet.

First there is the woods.

It is an eighty-acre patch of poplar. At one time it had been cleared land, a part of a small hundred-and-sixty-acre homestead, but the farmer who cleared the land had been driven out by the Depression of the 1930s. He had built a log house with two rooms and a loft and had tried to keep a family alive and happy on a hundred and sixty acres with eighty acres clear and eighty in brush and woods. But there was no market for anything the farmer grew, and he could not make enough for taxes, and so it went back to the state. And then back to nature. The poplars grew fast, and by the time of the hunt the trees were thirty feet high and the ground covered in hazel brush about waist high. The eighty acres can't be walked through in a straight line. The hunter must weave around the clumps of hazel, and it is hard because the ends of the bow snag and catch and the arrow shaft keeps banging against poplar trees, rattling and making enough noise to scare away any game within miles.

Any game but a deer—this deer, this special deer. But not yet.

There is the boy.

He hunts alone this time. Many times he has hunted this stand of woods with the other boys and taken grouse and rabbits with the blunts, walked through the woods in a line abreast. But this time Tip is sick and Wayne is on a trip and this has happened and that has happened, and he decided to come alone. He sometimes liked to hunt alone because he was alone so much of the time when he was in town because of his parents. He tries to have the right clothes, the right equipment, but there is no money, has never been any money, and so he must make do. He wears an old field jacket, so ragged it hangs almost in rags, but it is military green and seems to blend in and he thinks it is his lucky jacket because he was wearing it the day he got a shot at a twelve-point buck. He missed, but still he saw the buck, and though the shot went wide and missed he was of the thought that when hunting with a bow a miss was almost as important as hitting because actually hitting a deer seemed impossible—something in *Sports Afield* articles that always happened to somebody else.

He had many great misses. There was the twelve-pointer, and a spike buck that ran past him ten feet away, and a four-pointer he nearly stepped on and a six-pointer that stood perfectly still while he released a perfect, aimed shot that was heading exactly at the buck's heart but stuck in a two-inch sapling that stood in front of the deer. Misses all, arrows gone, skipping off tree limbs or rocks, flying away in small zips of light. So many misses that bow hunting for deer seemed not real to him—something done for fun alone; a kind of dance.

Until this day, this morning.

When it came, when it happened, it did not work the way it did in his dreams. There was a small clearing where the homestead cabin once stood. It had fallen in on itself and for the most part was a rotting mass of old logs and boards. But one wall still stood about four feet high, and as he approached the wall he caught a slight movement along the top of the wall out of the corner of his eye.

He froze, watching. Once he had seen a wolf hunting in a field. The wolf moved slowly, listening and watching, stopping absolutely still when there was any movement—a bird flying overhead, a mouse rustling in the grass, a bug—anything. The boy did the same when he hunted.

For a moment, for three breaths, he saw nothing and had nearly decided it must have been a small bird flitting by when it came again.

Along the top of the wall a line of fuzz seemed to move sideways. At first he couldn't make it work in his mind—a moving, horizontal fuzzy line. Then it moved again and he understood.

It was the back of a deer moving along the other side of the wall with its head down out of sight.

He held his breath, waiting, leaning forward as if his body were being pulled.

How far? he thought. Not fifteen, not even ten

yards. Feet. Twenty feet. The deer was moving along the wall not twenty feet from him, and with that thought, in that same instant, the deer appeared from in back of the logs.

It was a doe.

The light caught her as she came into view. She was losing the red summer color and had a brown coat, full and bushy so she looked almost unnaturally fat. The morning was cool and there were small jets of steam from her nostrils, little spurts that caught the morning sun and looked golden, almost like fire.

She had her head turned slightly away and had no knowledge, no idea the boy was there.

I'm so close, he thought—so close I could spit to her. He had never been this close to a live deer.

The bow.

He had completely forgotten the bow.

He let his eyes move down and saw that the arrow was still nocked to the string. Nothing in his thinking seemed to work right. I must do something, he thought—what? Oh yes, shoot. I must shoot. Still his arms did not move, seemed frozen.

But now things happened to take the decision away from the boy.

The doe had kept her head away from the boy but now she began to turn, the graceful neck arched, began to come around.

She would see him in a second, less, half a second. Less. No time.

Without thinking, without aiming or hesitating he raised the bow, drew the arrow to his chin and released—all in one motion.

There was a soft "thrummm" from the bow-string and the arrow left, flew from the bow, spiraling once and the boy saw the feathers seem to disappear against the side of the doe.

It didn't look like she'd been hit—the feathers just seemed to vanish.

She twitched slightly.

Not a jump. A small twitch, no more, and she turned to look at him, saw the boy standing, looked not just at him but up, into his eyes.

Then she turned away, walked slowly to the edge of the clearing and lay down in some tall grass there.

I missed her, he thought. Clean. For the moment he could not see her and he stepped forward to get a better view.

Then he saw the arrow.

It was lying on the ground six feet past where the doe was standing, just lying there, not buried in the grass or dirt.

From the point to the feathers it was completely red, totally covered with blood.

Oh, he thought. I hit her.

The red numbed him. He wasn't sure what he expected if he actually hit a deer. He always knew what to do when he missed a deer because he missed them all the time. When he missed he swore and made up an excuse—there was a crosswind, he shot too fast, the arrow planed on the point. A million excuses.

But he had no excuse for hitting a deer.

And he wanted one now badly.

He looked over in the grass, holding the bloody arrow, and saw the doe, watched the doe, and she looked at him once more, looked directly at him, into him, and he very much wanted an excuse for hitting the doe.

Then she turned away, turned her head away and stared into the clearing, ignoring him, stared through the clearing and through the woods and maybe through the sky, through everything, and she laid her head down—almost in sleep, the movement, though he knew better, knew that he had in less than a second ended something beautiful, something that could never be again, ended this doe— and she died. She laid her head down and took a last breath, in and out, pulled her back legs closer to her front and died.

Was no more.

Her world, the boy thought, *I have ended her world,* and the boy would live, would have a life and take a million breaths and eat and sleep and love and dance and have first things, first times, but not the doe.

She would have nothing. No world.

And he would never forget it; would remember everything, every aspect of it; would remember her color and the grass and the blood on the arrow and her last breath going out in steam, going out of her with her life—would remember the last of her for the rest of his life.

Duck Hunting

After grouse, after rabbits, after bow hunting for deer, but before the long winter hunts, there was duck hunting.

Sometimes it was walking along the river out of town, starting in the cold mornings, the rainy cold mornings of late October when nobody sane went outside.

Teal flew along the river, their wings whistling, and were difficult to hit because they flew so fast and never seemed to reveal themselves until it was too late to raise the old single-barrel sixteen-gauge and shoot.

Jump-shooting mallards was better. Wayne had a smokey-black Lab named Ike after the president, and he would retrieve with a lily-soft mouth no matter who shot the duck. North of town there were chains of swamps with open, small potholes of dark water where the mallards would sit. It was hard to walk because the peat under the swamp-grass was unfrozen and springy and frequently allowed a foot to go through down into the mud, where it tried to suck a boot off. But a rhythm could be felt after a time, and it was possible to move forward. Because the grass was so deep the mallards would be surprised, and it was while they were rising, their wings pounding to give them altitude—it was then that sometimes a shot could be taken, and Ike would watch with even brown eyes for the mallard to fall. At the moment it was hit, when it went from the beauty of a flying duck to the broken form of death —at that moment Ike would leap forward into the pothole and sometimes be waiting when the duck hit the water.

But there was an uncle . . .

Walk-hunting was fine except that it was limited and so clumsy that some of the art was lost.

But there was an uncle who had a duck-boat and an old truck and a rusty brown Chesapeake retriever named Robby, and the uncle and Robby took the boy out one morning to hunt ducks, and though the boy never hunted that way again it was in him and his mind from then on.

The uncle had just come back from fighting in Korea and would be in the boy's life for only one year before the uncle would move on to Montana, where he would hole up and think on what he had done and seen in Korea.

He loved the dog and took it with him everywhere, talked to it as if it were a person, and sometimes would even read to the dog out of books he carried that had strange-sounding names the boy could not understand, though there were several of them on the dashboard of the truck and the boy could read the titles on the spine. Titles like *The Collected Writings of Plato* and *Aristotelian Thinking*.

The boy did not sleep the whole night before and was up waiting when the uncle arrived at four o'clock.

It was pitch-dark and cold—so cold there was ice on the puddles left by rain during the night. The truck was a 1940 Ford with a cranky heater, but Robby was in the front seat with the uncle and climbed on the boy as soon as he got in the truck. The dog was warm and smelled of dog food and outside, and the boy cuddled with him while they drove north out of town to the flat swampy lakes that sat squat in the middle of the main migratory flight path.

At some point on the drive in the old truck through the dark morning the boy fell asleep with his face buried in the dog's neck-fur. He was awakened by the sound of the uncle talking.

"We'll work that stand of rice on the south end of the lake."

The voice was soft, even.

"Come in there quiet, before first light, and try

to catch the early-dawn movers like we did last time. . . ."

The boy nodded, but he felt the dog move and cock his ears and lean away and realized the uncle was talking to the dog and not him.

"May be some geese moving, too," the uncle said. "Most of them are already gone south but there might be a few." The uncle poured hot coffee from a thermos expertly, while driving, popped the cork back in the mouth of the thermos and then produced a half pint of Calvert Reserve from his duck-coat pocket and dropped a generous amount in the hot coffee. The smell of the whiskey on top of the hot coffee immediately filled the cab of the truck, but the boy pretended not to notice because he did not like drinking. To hide the smell of the whiskey he buried his nose in the dog's fur again.

The uncle spoke no more but sipped the coffee in silence while they drove for another half hour. Then he turned off the main road and killed the headlights and drove for ten or fifteen minutes in darkness so black the boy could see only a dim bulk of trees to the side of the track.

The dog knew where they were and became excited when the uncle stopped the truck.

Without speaking he climbed out of the truck and moved around to the rear. He pulled rubber boots out of the back end and jerked them on over his regular boots, then waited while the boy—who was already wearing rubber boots because that's all he had—came around the truck to help with the duck-boat.

The boat was twelve feet long, flat on the bottom and pointed at both ends so it would slide through the swamp-grass more easily. In the center was a seven-foot-long cockpit where two men and a dog could sit if they remained still and patient.

They put the boat in the water—or rather the uncle guided the boy, because it was still so dark he could see nothing—and the dog jumped in without having to be told.

The uncle brought two guns and handed the boy one—a sixteen-gauge Ithaca pump as old or older than he was—and put boxes of shells in the boat.

"Get in."

The boy was so excited that he tripped and stumbled and would have fallen had the uncle not caught him and helped him.

The boy moved to the front of the boat, and the uncle climbed in the back and laid his shotgun down and a large gunnysack down, stood and worked the pole with the steel expanding feet against the grass to propel the boat through the weeds and stands of rice.

It was still dark, but now the boy could see outlines, edges, and he watched ahead of the boat and made out the shape of a blind just before the boat bumped into it. The uncle poled back, moved the nose over, and worked slowly to the front of the blind. When the boat was in a small patch of clear water, he opened the sack and pulled out decoys, arranged them in a kind of fan, each held down with a lead sinker and a cord. Then he turned the boat and slid it back inside the blind, where he squatted down and laid the pole to the side on the grass.

"We'd better load—the light will come fast now when it comes."

He flipped his shotgun over, and the boy did the same with the Ithaca pump, loaded it with three high-base shells from the box on the floor of the boat and studied the weapon in the new morning light.

The boy had never seen such a gun. All the bluing was worn, but it had been kept in perfect shape and coated with a light film of fine oil that jumped to his fingers and somehow to his mouth and he could taste the steel, taste the bluing, taste all the hunts the gun had been on, taste the years of the gun.

He loaded it, and when he worked the pump to chamber a shell the action was so worn it almost worked itself, closed with a soft "snicking" sound that made him shiver and expect something he did not understand—some great adventure.

When the ducks came, the first ducks, they were high, just spots in the barely lighted sky, and the

uncle used a call to make the mallard feeding chuckle, and for a moment nothing happened. Then a small flock of eight or ten ducks set their wings and broke off in a long glide down toward the blind.

The boy could not stand it and when the ducks were still well out range he rose and fired, wobbling the boat and startling both the uncle and the dog.

The ducks veered away and the sudden explosion brought up hundreds of them that had been in the weeds around the boat. The boy stared, open-mouthed, while the uncle fired from a sitting position; once, twice, and two of the jumpers fell.

Before they hit the weeds Robby was over the side and heading for them. He brought one back within a minute—while the boy still stared—and went back for the other without being told. This one he found after working the weeds with his head down, belly-deep in swampwater, and carried it back with a wing flapping because the duck was still alive. The uncle quickly killed it and then turned to the boy and said, simply, "Maybe next time will be better."

And the next time was better.

A flock came in again high, specks in the gray-dawn sky, and the uncle called again, used the soft low chuckling sound from the call, and once more a group broke from the flock and started the glide down.

"I'll shoot left," the uncle whispered. "You right."

It was almost impossible to wait. The ducks seemed to hang in the air, caught on currents of wind that wouldn't let them down.

But they came, floating in a curve well out to the side to give them approach and landing room, and it seemed they would hit the water any second.

But this time the boy waited, watching the uncle out of the corner of his eye, waited until he couldn't stand it, and then waited even more until it seemed the ducks were going to land, were on their final approach, barely skimming the water near the decoys, and at last the uncle raised his shotgun and the boy did too and aimed at the duck on the right, aimed just in front of him and pulled the trigger.

Two ducks fell. The uncle had fired at exactly the same moment. The boy heard the pump work on the uncle's gun, did the same with his, and aimed at a mallard working to get high, flying straight up away from the water, and the boy fired and saw the duck break.

That's how it looked. How he thought of it. The duck broke. Its wings etched against the sky, broken and falling, the neck curved over backwards and he thought then, could not help but think then of the doe, the way the doe looked when she lay down in the grass and put her head over and down, and he had the first moment of true doubt; doubt that would plague him the rest of his life, moral doubt, growing doubt, doubt that ended childhood and in some measure ended the joy of hunting just as he had ended the duck and the doe.

Doubt that, ultimately, took him from the woods and the damp-smelling Chesapeake dog sitting in the gray morning, out into the real world, which he learned to live in but never learned to love as he had the world of hunting and fishing as a boy.

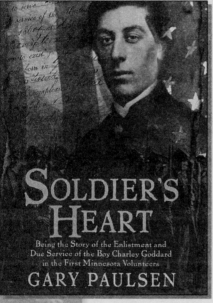